SHALLOW

TITLE PAGE:
At a later date, Nancy A. Osborn Jacobs sketched the Whitman mission as she remembered it at the time of the massacre, 1847. No. 1 was the Mission House; 2, Blacksmith Shop; 3, Emigrant House; 4, Grist Mill. The National Park Service has restored the pond, dikes, fencing, and apple orchard.

COVER:
Tomahas was the owner of the tomahawk now in the Oregon Historical Society Museum. It is said to be that used on Dr. Whitman.

INSIDE FRONT COVER:
Curtis photographed these Indians in what might have been Cayuse country. They may be Nez Percé or Cayuse. The one at right wears around his neck both beads and a medal, perhaps one of those presented to chiefs by Lewis and Clark.

Grave at Waiilatpu:
The Sagers' West

by

ERWIN N. THOMPSON

Oregon Historical Society
Revised Edition
1973

*acording to the best of my recolection, the above is a correct [view]
of the Whitman Mission buildings at the time of Massacre
N. A. Osborn*

Revised edition, 1973

Copyright, 1969, 1973
by
Oregon Historical Society

LC No. 77-110668
SBN 87595-024-8

Printed in U.S.A.
Glass-Dahlstrom Printers
Portland, Oregon

Preface

No one can live in the Pacific Northwest long before hearing about the Sagers. Television, radio, newspapers, and educators throughout the region have repeatedly brought the legend—if not the history—of this pioneer family to attention. One would have to look hard for a student who has not been assigned reading on the Sager family. Such attention is not surprising, for the story of this family covers almost every theme of the development of the Pacific Northwest: the Oregon Trail, missionaries, fur traders, pioneering, Indians, gold mining, and such dramatic episodes as massacre and Indian captivity.

Yet historians have left the Sager story to novelists. Some of the novels have been very popular, and some have been of low caliber. Together they have created a great myth about the Sagers that teachers have been passing on to generations of younger people. This myth tells us that the Sagers were a super-family, brave, strong, good, patriotic, and beyond any of the faults that beset ordinary people. The myth, of course, was put up as a model, a target at which young people should aim. How discouraging! All young people have feet of clay and most of them know that they are not perfect and never will be. The Sager story would have had much deeper meaning to them had they known that the Sagers were like themselves—complicated mixtures of many virtues and some weaknesses.

The most popular of the novels has been Honore Willsie Morrow's *On To Oregon*. Presented by Mrs. Morrow as history, this book has been reprinted many times, condensed in national publications, and plagiarized by a number of less creative writers. According to the plot, the seven Sagers, once orphaned on the trail, were forced by their traveling companions to turn back to the United States alone. But John, aided from time to time by Kit Carson, who performed magical accomplishments in traveling great distances in a flash, led his brother and sisters on to Oregon alone. Not only was John able to keep a four-months-old baby alive on the desert for weeks on end, he developed the belief that he was destined to save Oregon from Great Britain.

Recourse to fiction has never been necessary in telling the Sager story. The events that befell this family exceeded the scope of the imaginations of most story tellers. Yet, despite the wealth of adventure, the would-be historian faces one great problem, that of the scarcity of documents concerning the adult lives of the surviving Sagers. This absence of knowledge is particularly true of Henrietta's life from the time she went on the stage until her mysterious death. At times I thought I should end the story with the Sagers' release from Indian captivity. In the end, I took the narrative to the end of their lives. But the last chapter is merely an outline of their later years. Perhaps, some day, the material will be available that will fill in the many gaps.

Before I began this study I asked myself if the Sager story was worth the time and energy it would take in research and writing. I asked myself the same question when I had finished. In both instances the answer was in the affirmative. The work answered many of my own questions and fulfilled my own curiosity. The Sager story is high adventure filled with drama and excitement. The Sagers, although none of them shook the world, were a representative part of the human beings that formed the Oregon Country and all the endeavor and hope that have since emerged from these people. And finally, even Mrs. Morrow would approve; the Sagers as youngsters and as adults possessed a great strength of character; in the oldfashioned sense of the words, they were strong and brave. They were no stronger or braver, perhaps, than many thousands of others who cut their ties and traveled for six months to a new land without any hope of ever returning to the old. But the Sagers were dramatic representatives of the thousands.

The two thousand miles of the Oregon Trail were nothing in terms of the distances involved in today's space travel. In the 1840's however, the emigrants of the Oregon Trail were the space travelers of their time.

Acknowledgements

The National Park System has contributed greatly to this book. I first became interested in the Sagers when working as a park historian at Whitman Mission National Historic Site. I wrote most of the manuscript in a campground at Yosemite National Park, not being employed by the National Park Service at the time. If any of my neighboring campers of that summer should read this, they know now what that odd person was up to at his picnic table day after day. Much later, I made the necessary revisions in the manuscript at another National Park, Cape Hatteras National Seashore. Perhaps not everyone would choose a mountain for a writing room, but I did and am grateful that such an environment exists.

Encouragement and assistance from members of the National Park Service have made the way easier over the past several years as I worked on the Sagers when time and circumstance allowed. William J. Kennedy, Raymond Stickler, John Jensen, Robert Olsen, Dean Nicholas, and Robert Huntsman, all at one time or other at Whitman Mission NHS, have been most generous in helping me find the answers to many questions. Mrs. Glennis Shute, also at Whitman Mission, has been over the years a great builder of morale. She was never too busy to keep me informed by mail of any matter concerning the Sagers, including the names and addresses of descendants who visited the Mission.

Dr. John A. Hussey and Archeologist Paul J. F. Schumacher, both at the Western Region Office, National Park Service, San Francisco, have given me help over the years, especially in directing me toward potential sources. My thanks also go to Mrs. Marietta Schumacher, San Francisco, whose interest in the Sager story has been a steady source of inspiration.

Lawrence L. Dodd, Walla Walla, has expended many hundreds of hours of his time searching the Archives at Whitman College and in newspaper files for answers to my many questions. An excellent photographer, an enthusiastic searcher, Mr. Dodd has contributed greatly in the research on the Sagers. My thanks too to Mrs. Marylin Sparks, Librarian, Walla Walla, who undertook additional research in Walla Walla newspapers.

Mrs. M. Jeanne Gulick, formerly the Archivist, Whitman College, Walla Walla, answered my letters on the Sagers for nearly a decade. Her patience and generosity have been remarkable, and her constant attention to the subject of the Sagers has resulted in the discovery of a number of letters hitherto unknown. Thanks are extended both to Mrs. Gulick and to her husband, Bill Gulick, the noted author, who properly insisted that I rewrite and rewrite and never lose faith.

A number of historical societies in the Pacific Northwest contributed knowledge from their growing resources. My thanks go to Thomas Vaughan, Oregon Historical Society, and Merle W. Wells, Idaho Historical Society, and their staffs. Special thanks are extended to Miss Priscilla Knuth, as research associate and later as managing editor, Oregon Historical Society. Acknowledgment is made, too, for the aid of the Louis and Maud Hill Family Foundation and Western Imprints Fund of the Society for publication funds.

My thanks go also to the following people who greatly helped me in the preparation of this book: Robert G. Ferris and Frank B. Sarles, Jr., National Park Service, Washington, D.C., and Jerrie Ferris, Springfield, Va., who contributed greatly by reading the manuscript and offering valuable suggestions; and Majorie Bearss, Arlington, Va., who carefully prepared the index. The following persons made available illustrations and other materials: Nyle Miller, Director, Kansas State Historical Society, Topeka; Don Reynolds, Asst. Director, Saint Joseph Museum, Mo.; Homer L. Rouse, Superintendent, Scotts Bluff National Monument, Neb.; Lewis A. Eaton, Park Aid, Fort Laramie National Historic Site, Wyo.; Vance Orchard, Roving Reporter, *Walla Walla Union-Bulletin,* Wash.; Arley D. Jonish, Librarian, and Louise Humphrey, Audio-Visual Librarian, Penrose Memorial Library, Whitman College, Walla Walla, Wash.; and G. Donald Smith, Director of Libraries, Washington State University, Pullman, Wash.

The Arthur H. Clark Co. granted permission to make several short quotations from Clifford M. Drury's *First White Women Over the Rockies.*

A rare treat for me in the preparation of the manuscript was meeting two granddaughters of the Sagers: Mrs. Nancy D. Carpenter, San Francisco, granddaughter of Matilda, and Mrs. Sadie Collins Armin, Sioux Falls, granddaughter of Catherine. These two ladies allowed me a three-and-a-half-hour interview in Mrs. Armin's hotel room in San Francisco. The maid had not yet made the bed when I arrived. Both ladies apologized and quickly "spread it up," Mrs. Carpenter saying, "Grandmother Matilda would not have approved of this" poor housekeeping. I knew at that moment that I was with friends and that the interview would be profitable. Indeed it was. Since then Mrs. Carpenter and Mrs. Armin have graciously responded to long letters from me; at one time Mrs. Carpenter patiently answered no fewer than 92 questions.

A third Sager granddaughter, Mrs. Celista Collins Platz, Seattle, granddaughter of Catherine, also has generously loaned all the Sager material in her collections, including copies of her grandmother's scrapbooks and correspondence.

To all these people and others not mentioned by name I owe thanks. If the book had been written without their help, it would have been far less complete.

ERWIN THOMPSON

Contents

	Page
Preface	v
Acknowledgements	vii
Born to Wander	1
Wagon Train	10
Seven Orphans	23
"Your Children Have Come"	31
Whitman Mission	43
A New Life	59
"As If They Were My Own"	68
Tension	81
Massacre	92
Captivity	104
"A Free People"	115
Interlude	125
A New Life	129
Footnotes	156
Bibliography	170
Index	174

Illustrations

St. Joseph, Missouri, 1850	6
John Minto and Michael T. Simmons	11
Buffalo hunting on the Plains	17
Courthouse and Jail rocks	19
Scotts Bluff and the Oregon Trail	20
Fort Laramie (Fort John), 1846	22
Devil's Gap on the Sweetwater	24
Three Islands Crossing, Snake River	32
Sagebrush plains and Fort Boise, 1849	34
Descending the Blue Mountains toward Umatilla	37
Marcus and Narcissa Whitman	38
W. H. Gray	47
Old Lapwai mission	50
Elkanah and Mary Walker	52
Tshimakain mission, 1843-44	56
Whitman mission, 1845	64
Memorial Shaft Hill, adjacent to the Whitman mission	66

Cayuse Indian mat lodges	87
Grist mill ruins, Whitman mission	89
Indians attacking Dr. Whitman	94
Tiloukaikt and Tomahas	96
Whitman mission house plan, 1840	100
Father J. B. A. Brouillet	106
Five Crows, Cayuse chief	109
Fort Walla Walla, 1853	118
Methodist mission at the Dalles	120
Peter Skene Ogden	122
Joseph L. Meek	127
Catherine and Henrietta Sager	130
Great Grave, Waiilatpu and inscribed stone	132
Anniversary observation of Whitman massacre	135
Catherine, Elizabeth and Matilda, 1897	137
NPS Visitor Center at Whitman mission site	141
Lewis M. Hazlitt and Matilda Sager Hazlitt	149
Walla Walla, Washington, 1889	154

Map

The Sagers' route west, 1844	28-29

SHALLOW GRAVE
AT WAIILATPU:
THE SAGERS' WEST

Emigrants Crossing the Plains.
From an 1869 engraving.

Born to Wander

Henry Sager acquired his wanderlust through precept. Three generations of his ancestral Sagers, spelled Seeger in the old country, had already partaken in the westward marches of the Americans. The first of these, George Sager, Henry's great-grandfather, came from Germany about 1738, possibly from the Odenwald district of Hessen.[1] The eighteen-year-old German had crossed the storm-gray Atlantic and walked ashore amid the bustlings of the Quakers of Philadelphia.

Whatever his reasons, George did not stay long in this port city. Moving inland, he settled in Lancaster County. Before very much time passed he married and, in 1744, at age 25, became the father of a boy. This son, whom his parents also christened George, inherited his father's restlessness. Before the century was out, with a family of his own, he moved southward from Lancaster County to Virginia. The family records of this move are scanty and they do not tell if George, Jr., traveled the famous Great Philadelphia Wagon Road to his new home in the western part of Virginia, as did many of Pennsylvania's early settlers. Regardless of their route, the Sagers' timing made them a thread in that great tapestry of movement that crossed the ocean to the clearings of Pennsylvania, then southward through the gaps and across the streams to make new clearings in the blue-green hills of Virginia and beyond.

Here in this newest place, George's son, Christian, married Maria Elizabeth Shover and began the fourth generation. On October 8, 1805, a son was born in Loudoun County and, in the following spring, he was baptized Heinrich in the New Jerusalem Lutheran church in Lovettsville. In that same year, 1806, the call of the virgin land in the West reached Christian, and he led the family across the Alleghenies to make a new home in the Ohio Valley.

The maturing of Henry, as he was called, in this fast-growing land and his subsequent travels would have been lost in the anonymity of the past had he not eventually sired seven children. The number was not unusual, but these seven were to be the thread that linked quiet Henry with the legends of Oregon. In his twenty-fifth year, an important time in strength and manhood, Henry took for his wife a young woman named Naomi Carney. She was the prim but gentle daughter of a Baptist preacher who had also come from the east to pay homage to the Ohio. Before her marriage, Naomi had been a school teacher.[2]

For the next few years Henry dutifully farmed his land in Union County and fulfilled his role as husband. In 1831, Naomi bore the first of their seven children, a son whom she named John after her own father. Two years later their second child was born. This too was a boy, Francisco. This may have seemed an unusual name for an eastern preacher's daughter to favor. Perhaps because of an awareness of this, he forever afterward went by the name of Francis or Frank. It is possible that a Francisco, an established surname in Virginia, had married into either her or Henry's family.

There were no more boys. In April 1835 came Catherine, the first of five girls. She was named for her grandmother, Catherine Carney. A second daughter, Elizabeth, arrived in July 1837, along with the Panic of that year. Hard times fell upon the Ohio Valley, and Henry and his neighbors began to pay heed to the stories of richer, unsettled land farther west. Along with many others, he concluded that the tillable soil of the Ohio was becoming too crowded. If the stories one heard were right, a man had a better chance farther west where there was space to be an individual and to watch one's family grow with the young country.

Shortly after the birth of his third daughter in 1839, an imp of a girl named Matilda Jane after whom nobody knows, Henry packed his earthly possessions and left Ohio behind forever.[3] He stopped in Indiana, but it did not answer to his dreams, or perhaps he meant it to be just a resting place. While there, Naomi had the opportunity of visiting her mother who was then living with a sister, Hannah Price, in White County.[4] The ferment to push on to the frontier had affected Henry, just as it had many others, and his soul could not find peace here among the multitudes. Having little to lose, he found it an easy decision to travel still farther west.

In that same year the Sagers found themselves in Missouri. This was as far west as a man took his family in 1839. There was nothing beyond except the endless plains and the Indians. No one knew how to tame the treeless prairie yet. It was still called the Great American Desert. The American settler was yet a man of the forest; to him the great grassy sweeps seemed barren and forbidding. True, still farther on, two thousand miles away, there was a mystic unmeasured land called Oregon. But that strange name did not quite yet figure in a man's dreams.

Henry's first home in Missouri was in the eastern part of the state. Perhaps he did not mean to stop here very long. In any case, 1840 found him in Platte County on the western border of the state. He settled down to plant tentative roots in this new home. Besides farming, Sager developed a blacksmith business. He had "a wide reputation for ingenuity," Catherine recalled, "and I have heard neighbors remark that they believed that Henry Sager had made everything in common use but a saddle." She added, "they believed he could make one if he would set about it."[5] But as Henry tilled his soil and worked in the smithy, strange stories began to flicker up and down the frontier about a true paradise — the Oregon Country.

These stories about a rich land, claimed by both Great Britain and the United States but not yet belonging to either, were heard by eager ears. Ever since 1837 the nation had been sunk in a heart-rending depression. But slowly better times were coming about. By the time Henry had lived in Platte County two years, farmers were beginning to find a market for their pork. No longer did they give their bacon to the river boats to burn as fuel, or throw away wheat at ten cents a bushel. Prices went up and there was new hope in the land.[6]

Many of the frontier farmers were in no hurry to forget the years of suffering. They were an eager audience for stories that promised an end to famine. Tales of the paradise called Oregon suited the needs of the times. These stories, barely a whisper at first, passed from lip to ear and became a whirlwind. Rare was the man who could pick out the few gems of truth in the wonders he heard. Still rarer was the man who wanted to. Who wished to dispute the dream of a fabulously rich, unsettled land where it was summer all the time? Who bothered to note that the only women ever to cross the plains and the mountains were a handful of wives of starry-eyed missionaries? Who doubted but what the land would become American and he who got there first would get the best? Nobody who counted.

But as long as the depression had lasted only the dreams had moved. The people did not. Men could scarcely give their land away. A family man had not been able to raise the price of a wagon, oxen, food, and all the necessities required before even crossing the Missouri.[7] Yet the dream had persisted. Now, as men slowly regained their faith in their society, the time to travel came closer.

It began in 1842. Before then a trickle of fanatics, who could not bear to wait, had plunged recklessly onto the prairie. But in this spring over one hundred men, women, and children said their farewells to the familiar and crossed the wide Missouri. In 1843, almost one thousand people joined in what was to be called later the Great Migration, and ate each other's dust as they tracked the setting sun. The Oregon Trail was now born in fact, for this train took its wagons of household goods all the way to the Columbia and down that River of the West to the Willamette Valley. There the bright bubbles of fantasy burst. But the reality alone was enough to make a man feel he had done well. Oregon was a rich young land, big enough to satisfy the most restless soul.[8]

Henry Sager became a part of all this. His dream was a part of the great one, and he entered the vortex of this swirling movement like a twig in a spring flood. In the autumn of 1843 he sold his farm and blacksmith business and moved his family to St. Joseph on the Missouri.[9] By now he and Naomi counted six in their brood; Hannah Louise had been born in 1841.

The father of St. Joseph was Joseph Robidoux who was of that lusty but diminishing clan, the fur traders and mountain men.[10] When the Sagers arrived, St. Joseph was yet a struggling, new-born village hoping to attract a rich share of the new overland travel. Prior to 1844, nearly all explorers, traders and would-be emigrants had outfitted themselves at Westport Landing and Independence, mudholes farther downstream. But

Robidoux and others like him bet, correctly, that emigrants would look upon St. Joseph as a good jumping-off place. Travelers on the Missouri boats would be able to stay on board the steamers an extra two days. This in turn would mean four days less on the prairie once their wagons were underway.[11]

At St. Joseph that winter, Naomi Sager seems to have been of a mixed mind. Her daughters later recalled that she complained of having traveled westward for years. Was it not time to settle down to the reality of feeding six hungry children? Still, she had heard of the healthful climate on the Pacific Coast, and her tired body yearned for that. But did they have to move in 1844? Could they not wait another year? Naomi was pregnant again. But Henry reacted like a man saved by a religious experience. Human weakness was not to be allowed to interfere; it had to be 1844.[12]

When the early spring rains brought freshness to the land, the emigrants of that year began to gather along the Missouri. Dozens, soon hundreds of people arrived to prepare for the greatest undertaking of their lives. By March, St. Joseph was a hustling frenetic town, a community of transients whose accumulating excitement became contagious.

The men met in small groups in front of the blacksmiths' shops and argued the merits of mules and oxen. In the end most would choose oxen.[13] The horse traders worked feverishly to get the best prices for their stock. The fires of the shops glowed throughout the lengthening days as blacksmiths hammered furiously to meet the demand for ox and horse shoes, wheel rims, and all the products of their trade. Women pondered, decided, and changed their minds on how many pounds of flour they would need. They wept when they realized there would not be room in the wagons for the fine old bureaus and beds they had loved for years. They sorted, discarded, and prayed over their belongings. And still they would take too much. The trail would be littered with heirlooms from end to end.

Life was too young and hope too high for these wanderers to heed the warnings that the sleek oxen and the oiled wagons would wear out, the green grasses would turn brown and sparse, and the hills would grow longer. These were lessons for later. For now, husbands and wives argued where to put the chamber

pots and how to store the musket powder. And around and over the wagons swarmed the multitude of children, frantic with excitement, screaming with life. They could scarcely conceive of the event but they knew it was a great time to be alive.

March gave way to April and the virginity of another spring along the Missouri blessed the land. Last year's dead grass still responded to the breezes, but its dry stalks guarded the first green shoots of the new life. At St. Joseph the families made themselves as ready as they would ever be. One by one the wagons left the village and struggled up to Capler's Landing, six miles north. This was the true point of departure.

Along with those at St. Joseph, men at other jumping-off places hastened to shoe the last ox, to put the last barrel on the wagon, and to wave goodbye to well-wishers. There were four separate trains this year. Farther up the Missouri than even St. Joseph, at Council Bluffs, the Stephens-Townsend-Murphy party headed west along the Platte River. This party was to split at Fort Hall on the Snake River many hundreds of miles farther west—many of them going on to Oregon, but a small and determined group heading toward Mexico's California.[14]

A large caravan starting from Independence this year was captained by Nathaniel Ford and guided by a famed ex-mountain man, Moses "Black" (Major) Harris. Traveling along the north bank of the Platte was the fourth train, a small party under the command of John Thorp. This caravan was following the same route traveled by the American Board missionaries, Marcus Whitman and Henry Spalding, in 1836.[15] Three of the caravans —Ford's, Thorp's, and the wagons from St. Joseph—remained fairly close to one another in the western reaches of the great plains, and Moses Harris became a general guide to all three.[16]

No one stopped to count how many people started for Oregon that year, although nearly all of them tried to total them up afterward. A census of the St. Joseph group before it was fully formed showed: "1 minister, 1 lawyer, 1 millwright, 3 millers, 1 tailor, 2 cabinet makers, 5 carpenters, 1 ship-carpenter, 3 blacksmiths, 1 cooper, 1 tailoress, 1 wheelwright, 2 shoemakers, 1 weaver, 1 gunsmith, 1 wagonmaker, 1 merchant, and the rest farmers." The report said that there were "48 families, 108 men (60 of whom are young men), 323 persons, 410 oxen,

This 1850 sketch of St. Joseph, Missouri, shows how quickly the town had grown in the six years after the Sagers left here for the Oregon Country. (Courtesy St. Joseph, Mo., Museum.)

160 cows (16 of which are team cows), 143 young cattle, 54 horses, 11 mules, and 72 wagons. The number of horned cattle is 713 head. Many men from the adjoining counties are on their way to join us." In this and the other trains at least 700 people reached Oregon and perhaps another 200 saw the shores of California.[17]

While the various trains were never far from one another, they did not unite into a single organization. They learned swiftly, as had the travelers of 1843 and as future trains were to learn each year, that survival on the plains was dependent upon small encampments generously scattered over considerable distances. Once spring passed into summer, there would be little enough grass for even small camps. Besides the problem of forage, there was the billowing dust cloud that signaled the passage of a wagon train over the prairie. Even in small groups, those at the end of the processions suffered greatly from the clinging alkali dust that conquered all precautions. "Eating dust" was always a cause for argument; in one large train it would have caused violence.

Although there was always the possibility of attack from hostile bands of Indians, this scourge of later emigrants was not yet the pattern of the plains. The Indians did not yet feel threatened, just curious. Nonetheless, in this year and in the rest of the 1840's, it was common for the separate trains to pace themselves so that they were within a day or two of one another should some terrible emergency arise.

At Capler's Landing friends and acquaintances now came to see the wanderers cross the Missouri, going to God knew where. Tears were shed, hugs exchanged, and sadness felt. No one could quite realize why the parting had to be. Those not yet infected with the Oregon fever could not understand why anyone felt he *had* to go. But those who had the fever in their minds could no longer comprehend old friends who seemed satisfied to remain behind. Catherine Sager experienced the mixed emotions of the parting: "Some wept for departing friends, and others at the thoughts of leaving all they held dear for a long and uncertain journey." The children had their own concerns; they "wept for fear of the mighty waters that came rushing down and seemed as though it would swallow them up." Impressionable Catherine remembered, "It was a sad company that crossed over the Missouri River that bright spring morning."[18]

The sadness was real but sympathy was useless. These were free men starting on a Great Adventure, and they knew they were making history. Hard times lay ahead, but these people knew they would discover beyond the setting sun the source of all rainbows—a land of plenty and of power. For many, the coming months of travel were to be the most enjoyable experience of their lives. For a few, tragedy would dominate the trail. The Sagers, indeed all families, assumed they were to be among the blessed.

On the far side of the river, the wagons from St. Joseph straggled into an agreed-upon rendezvous. The intention had been to hold a council here in order to organize the train and to elect leaders. Some wagons had crossed the Missouri weeks, even months, earlier, finding it more convenient to await spring and their companions on the western side than in St. Joseph. But now there was too much excitement and restlessness for coherent organization to take place. Even before latecomers arrived, wagons started pulling out in a race to be first on the trail. The call "To Oregon" threatened to defy man's instinct for order.

Twenty-five miles farther west was the Nemaha Indian Agency. This was the last chance to obtain the services of a blacksmith. All the wagons stopped and the travelers took care of things forgotten in the rush, or simply stared at the few poor specimens of Indians present. Then, moving on, the wagons eventually rolled into camp on the great prairie, already beyond everything the people had held familiar. No longer could the organization of the train be put off. It was now May, and the road to Oregon lay gleaming in the fresh land soaked with the rains of spring.

Wagon Train

On May 20, the men settled down finally to the serious business of organizing. Like Henry Sager, most of them came from the frontier settlements of Missouri. Although there was a scattering of Yankees and New Yorkers in the caravan, most of the men or their fathers had been born in Kentucky, Tennessee, Virginia, or North Carolina.[19] They were not highly educated but they knew at first hand the practices of the militia and they attempted now to combine military trappings with their attitudes of unrestrained independence. They followed the precedents of previous trains by organizing themselves along military lines. The caravan felt that if enough of a military aura were adopted, then the necessary discipline would be forthcoming and there would be an effective defense should Indians attack. Bancroft said of these 1844 migrants, "Their tendencies were more toward military glory than pride of statesmanship."[20]

The men had already agreed that the commander should be Cornelius Gilliam. It was around him that the travelers had focused their ambitions. And the impetuous, dashing, daring, and not too bright "General" Gilliam was not one to hide his command capabilities. He had had some real military experience in the Black Hawk and Seminole wars, but his leadership was to be severely tested before the Rockies were reached.[21] To assist him, a quiet determined man, Michael Simmons, was elected as colonel. Simmons was not to cut much of a swath under Gilliam, but much later he and a few associates were to be daring enough to begin American settlement north of the Columbia, in the very lap of the Hudson's Bay Company's realms.[22]

For ease of travel and control, the train, which had been bravely christened the "Independent Colony,"[23] was divided into four companies, each with its own captain.[24] General Gilliam's brother-in-law, Captain William Shaw, from North Carolina and whom all the children called "Uncle Billy," was elected to command the company the Sager wagon was in. In contrast to

[10]

Young Englishman John Minto's comments describe the overland journey of the Sager family. This 1862 photo was taken when Minto was a sober member of the Oregon legislature. Michael T. Simmons, right, was a more prominent member and officer of the 1844 train. (OHS Collections.)

Gilliam, William Shaw was a wise, sober man, perhaps the best of those elected to command that year.[25] He and Sager had a high regard for each other and Shaw's friendship was to prove its value in the months ahead.

Another of the company commanders was Robert Wilson Morrison. He too was a good friend to Henry Sager and a man of better than usual leadership ability.[26] In the latter half of the trip west, the Morrison and Shaw companies were to remain particularly close to each other and both were to assist the Sager family during the desperate times ahead.

In general, Shaw, Morrison, Sager and all the others were good family men of rough exteriors. They mixed a spirit of adventure with a sense of responsibility toward their families. One of the young bachelors of the train, John Minto, an Englishman most recently from Pittsburgh, Pennsylvania, later wrote of them, "They were not a reading people, a prevailing ambition among them was to be the most western members of their respective families and to call no man master."[27]

Along with the families was a number of young single men out to make their names and fortunes. Many of these owned little more than the clothes they wore and their horses. Carrying few supplies, they attached themselves to the wagons. In return for their board they assisted in driving the oxen, herding the loose cattle, or hunting fresh meat. Minto, who hired himself to Captain Morrison, described his own brief preparations for the 2,000-mile adventure in the words, "Got me a nice new rifle." He continued, "I also laid in a supply of ammunition, purchasing five pounds of powder, twenty-five pounds of lead, one dozen boxes of percussion caps, five pounds of shot, and one gross of fishhooks, and lines to match; also I bought two pocket knives, two sheath knives, a hatchet to answer for a tomahawk, and an axe." With this armory and little else, he set out to conquer the West. Another young man in the caravan, James W. Marshall, had no idea that before long he would discover a great gold field in California.[28]

But that waiting land seemed very far away during the first days of travel. From the Indian Agency to the Platte River, heavy rains attacked the wagons daily. This was the year of a great flood throughout the eastern prairies, surpassing in its rage even the destructive floods of modern times, including the disastrous rains of 1951.[29] Day and night torrential rains tore at the canvas and battered the plodding oxen. Man and beast pulled themselves through unending miles of mud. The tributaries of the Kansas River overflowed their banks. Each crossing of these raging streams became a time of danger.

The women and children sought damp refuge under the leaking canvasses and listened to the wheels, in mud to their hubs, suck at the earth as they rolled onward. Even the high spirits of the children began to pall under the incessant storms. Where had the pleasures and joys of the first days gone? Huddled under wet blankets, shivering from cold that threatened to leave them forever chilled, they wished they were home again. Catherine could never forget these rains "that lasted for days and deluged everything." On one occasion, "The river near which we were encamped rose and overflowed its banks, until we had to move back nearly a day's journey. Water ran through the tent, and the bedclothes were saturated with water." To add to the travelers' misery, "the sun would not shine out enough during the day to dry the bedding."[30]

But even these rains did not last forever. There were days when the sun did break out and the emerald land shot forth the light of diamond oceans of moisture. The children climbed from the wagons and romped on the prairie. The men galloped across the rolling land in pursuit of whatever small animals happened to be near. With much head-shaking and shrill talk, the women attempted to dry the bedding before the next rain. Again it was good to be alive here and now. Soon the caravan would reach the Platte, the muddy stream that uncoiled all the way from the Rockies. Farther up that river would be the great bison herds. And every mile traveled, in rain or shine, made the figure 2,000 a little smaller — but very little. It took these emigrants almost three months to reach Fort Laramie, only 550 miles from St. Joseph. Nagging their thoughts was the worry that they must reach Oregon before winter swept over the western mountains.

To add to his own particular load of worries, Henry Sager was not a very good manager of oxen. Catherine remembered those first days of the journey wryly: "Father's outfit consisted of one large wagon; to this he had two yoke of well-broken oxen; the rest were young and unbroken, and as he was not used to driving he had much difficulty." Captain Shaw came to Sager's aid: "he [Shaw] lit into the oxen with stones until Father fearing for his own safety ran away." But the oxen quickly submitted when they "found that they had some one to deal with who knew his business."[31]

The oxen were only one of Henry's worries at the moment. Naomi's time for birth was close. Although the two of them had been through the experience six times, this was different. The wagons had already lost too much time because of the rains; he could not expect the whole train to stop for very long should Naomi have trouble. And he could not afford the risks of staying behind alone.

In a downpour on Thursday evening, May 30, the drenched wagons reached the flooded Nemaha River, near the present town of Seneca, Kansas, and the caravan camped on the near bank. During the night, Mrs. Shaw and Mrs. Morrison were hurriedly called to the Sager tent. There in the damp canvas shelter, Naomi gave birth to her seventh child. At the next dawn the rain was still falling. Dismayed by the flooded stream, the emigrants decided not to try crossing the river until noon, hoping that the sky would clear.

During that morning of May 31, E. E. Parrish noted in his diary, "This day a frolic in Mr. Sagers famelly." Another traveler wrote that an "important event occurred which was the addition of another member to Mr. Sager's family by the birth of a daughter." There were to be other "frolics" in other families before the journey ended, but Henry Sager's daughter was the first. The sky did clear by noon and the heavy wagons crossed the turbid stream. But the Sager wagon did not move. The birth had not been easy and Naomi was in great pain. Across the river, the caravan waited impatiently into the next day, until she and the baby could be moved safely. Parrish noted the growing anxiety to get on the trail again. June 1, "We are camped to wate for Mr. Sager, whose wife is sick   hope she will soon be well agan." June 2, "Camp ordered to remain stationary, to awate the recovery of Mrs Sager. She is reported very sick." In the afternoon of the same day he wrote, "Report sais Mrs. Sager is better, & that the camp will be ordered off, in the morning. Yes, yes, all true."[32]

Henry's wagon crossed the Nemaha and, on the morning of June 3, the migrants broke camp and pushed on toward another horizon. Bounced and jolted by the rutted prairie, Naomi lay as still as possible in her husband's wagon and held her newborn in her arms. Despite Parrish's optimistic report, she was not well and was never to recover fully. Her earlier worries about the journey were now realities. Despite the help of his neighbors and his older children, Henry's burdens lay heavily upon him.

The birth was but one of the multitude of events occurring in the train. As the days passed, the private lives of the members of the caravan continued much as if they were still in a Missouri village. There were marriages, births, deaths, gossip, and all the events that make a lifetime. A few days after the Sager frolic another kind of excitement broke out when two young men got into an argument. One of them, Clark Eads, attempted to shoot his adversary. He was lucky, for his shot missed. Judged under the provisions of the unwritten laws of the prairie, Eads was lectured to and either bound over for good behavior, or staked out in the sun from eleven a.m. until sunset, depending upon the authority.[33] Many weeks later his harried mother was to hold Naomi Sager's newborn in her arms in a grim struggle to keep the baby alive.

July 4 dawned bright and clear in a fitting manner. Mindful of the nation's anniversary and the past weeks of rain, General Gilliam ordered the holiday be observed by "A rest for the cattle, wash day for the women, and a day to hunt for the men."[34] At least the cattle and the men would enjoy the occasion. As the warm sun flooded the big sky, the land dried off its sparkle. After the usual breakfast of sowbelly, slam-johns, and hot biscuits, the women began the task of drying out the bedding, boxes, and barrels. The older children helped their fathers get away for the hunt, wanting more than anything in the world to ride along. Naomi Sager was not able to do much this day. For her the great thing was to rest in the shade of the tent instead of being torn in pain in the back of the wagon.

The cows were milked, dresses and underclothing scrubbed, and inventories of food made. Each woman opened her flour, coffee, sugar, and salt containers to the dry air. Then she made notes in her mind of the amount of pepper, tea, spices, and saleratus left. The rice, beans, corn meal, and dried fruit were sorted for spoilage. At noontime she and her children dipped leftover biscuits in molasses and ate a hasty but satisfying snack.[35] In the afternoon the men returned. If they had been lucky there would be a little fresh meat for supper. While the women busied themselves preparing this meal over a fire of wood carefully carried from the last grove of cottonwood along some creek bottom, the men opened the tar buckets and greased the axles of their wagons with a mixture of resin and grease. They painted gutta-percha on the canvas to make it a little more waterproof. The hickory bows, doubletrees, and whippletrees were checked for damage. Spare parts were brought out from the depths of the wagons.[36] They cleaned their muskets and hung them up behind the front seats. And in the lowering sun's glow they probably dreamed of the good times coming when they would meet the buffalo herds.

There was no time for games on this holiday, but the tradition of festivities was brightened by the evening marriage of Mary King to John Kindred. There were even fireworks of a sort when John's father heard it rumored that Miss King was a woman of ill fame. Although the solemn ceremony had already been performed by the Reverend Mr. Cave, "the Young Mans father, on learning the fact vetoed the thing by threatning to shute his son if he bedded with her. John knew his father & acted acordingly, so they never bedded together."[37]

Then, as dusk came on and all was ready for the morrow, the calm evening air carried the sounds of laughter and merriment. The emigrants sat about their small fires while stardust filled the sky. They sang the songs that bespoke optimism and hope. Families visited one another's fires and the community enjoyed a spell of good times. Catherine Sager described this ending of a good day, "There were several musical instruments in the company; and these sounded out clear and sweet on the evening air while gay talk and merry laughter went on around the camp fire."[38] Perhaps on such an evening Naomi was able to sit up for a while watching her children grow sleepy in the fire's glow. Only a few more months and they would be in Oregon.

On July 7, the travelers got their first view of the Platte River and the "Coasts of Nebraska."[39] Like all others seeing it for the first time, they made terrible jokes about the river: "It's a mile wide and an inch deep." "I wanted a drink so I took my knife and cut out a piece." Now, too, they saw prairie dogs for the first time. Man and beast stared at each other with solemn curiosity. Then, July 11, the travelers saw the first buffalo. The instant the great dumb lords of the plains were spotted, men grabbed their rifles and their best horses and were off in a plume of dust. Henry Sager rode with them.

Out on the prairie strange things began to happen. A few men retained their wits and pursued the herd only long enough to get fresh meat. Others went berserk and in wild recklessness engaged in an orgy of killing. Bleeding carcasses disfigured the prairie landscape. Not until darkness halted their madness did they return to the train. Arguments ran through the caravan like a range fire when the camp awoke the next morning. Part

[16]

Buffalo hunting scene on the plains, from Henry J. Warre's painting (1844-45). Men of the 1844 wagon train gave chase in this manner when they first spotted a buffalo herd.

of the train wanted to move on; there was no time to waste in buffalo killing. The rest, led by Gilliam himself, insisted the train remain in camp to allow another day's chase. The latter group won out when it was discovered that in the preceding day's wildness, few had dressed the meat properly and nearly all of it was spoiled. The train would have to remain in camp until more meat was brought in. The slaughter continued throughout this second day.

That night, angry meetings were held as the men drifted back into camp. By nightfall the protest had reached a crescendo. The second-in-command, Colonel Simmons, resigned. A new election replaced him with another, but morale and discipline were shattered. Despite his failure to control his instincts, Gilliam managed to retain the position of command, if not the actual power. He made a thrilling speech in which he promised the exact execution of military law in the future. But it was a hollow victory. It was clear from the voting that many no longer had confidence in his abilities as their leader.[40] The wanton killing of the past two days deeply disturbed those men who had learned frugality out of necessity. E. E. Parrish was greatly upset by the slaughter: "God forgive us for such a wast & save us from ignorance, as would lead to symilear results."[41]

As the caravan creaked along the arid bank of the Platte, the mutterings grew ever louder. Sensing the growing dissatisfaction, Gilliam resigned his command two days later. Gloom and black doubts hovered over the train, but no new elections were held. From then on, the St. Joseph train traveled without a commander. The captains of the companies assumed greater responsibilities and, in effect, each led his own small wagon train from that time forward. Parrish described the climax of the dissension: "A call together of the men, an abusive speach by the General, and his resignation. . . ." Mournfully he concluded, "Now we are in companies only . . ., this is a gloomy day to my minde." During the coming weeks, William Shaw and Wilson Morrison held their companies together with firm, fair hands.[24]

By this time, the Ford wagon train, from Independence, was traveling close to the St. Joseph group. James Clyman, a member of Ford's group, wrote in his diary that his train passed Gilliam's people on July 16, while Gilliam's companies moved ahead again on July 17. Three days later Clyman wrote: "4 days since we overtook Mr Gilhams company of Oregon Emigrants & yesterday an arrangement was entered into for the traveling in the neare vicinity of each other & encamping nofurther apart than necessary for the good of our stock so that our entire company makes 96 Teams wagons & occupies with loose stock & all more than two miles of tolerably close column."[43]

After crossing the wide, dangerous looking, but shallow South Fork of the Platte in the middle of July, the companies plodded along the North Fork toward the Rocky Mountains. One day, as Naomi was lying as usual in the wagon, the wheels on one side suddenly ran up on a ledge. Before the horrified Henry could do anything, the wagon tipped over on its side. Fearfully, he dug through the jumble to reach his family. The canvas "was removed, and the children were taken out and found to be unhurt." Catherine's dress had been torn off "Leaving nothing but the waist and a strip of the hind breath." Sager, who had been walking, had his face skinned when the wagon bows brushed past him. Naomi was seriously injured

[18]

Courthouse and Jail rocks, with Jail Rock (west) in foreground.
(George Grant photo, courtesy National Park Service.)

and "a tent was set up and Mother carried into it, where for a long time she lay insensible." Was there to be no end to hurt and sickness? There was not time to rest quietly to allow the flesh to recuperate. The days were passing too swiftly. The emigrants felt an urgency to hasten that was sharper now than when Naomi had had her baby. The wagon was righted, its goods repacked, and the injured woman was placed inside once again. To her, the cry "On, On" was becoming a call of pain.[44]

On July 25, the emigrants passed Court House Rock. Farther ahead they could see the famed Chimney Rock, but they did not pass this landmark until the 27th. Next loomed the massive block known as Scott's Bluff, beyond which the travelers got their first dim view of real mountains — the Laramie. The people of this year duly noted all these sentinels of the plains as did all others before and after them.

Three days later, July 30, Catherine Sager, the oldest of the five girls, was riding on the big seat at the front of the wagon. During the months of travel she had sat here often and had

Scotts Bluff on the right. Looking west on the Oregon Trail, which passed through the gap in the center. (George Grant photo, courtesy National Park Service.)

become adept at climbing on and off as the lumbering wagon rolled slowly onward. When she became tired of sitting she would jump over the side and walk next to the oxen or explore off to the side of the trail discovering new flowers, rocks, and all the things that attract a nine-year-old.

Deciding to walk, Catherine stood up and braced herself for the leap to the ground. She jumped, her long dress fluttering behind her. The dress caught on an ax handle sticking out from under the canvas. Catherine's slender body turned over in the air, the dress tore loose, and the girl fell to the ground. The huge creaking wheel of the wagon rolled toward her, over her thin leg, and on.

Henry stopped the oxen and gathered his daughter in his arms. Sick to his heart, he examined the twisted awkward leg and in a broken voice exclaimed, "My dear child, your leg is broken all to pieces." Elizabeth Sager never forgot the shock of seeing her oldest sister lying there with her leg "shivered all to pieces."[45]

Other wagons came to a halt and people gathered around the injured girl. There was no doctor in Shaw's company and Henry would not let anyone touch his daughter's leg. Someone recalled that a German emigrant, Dr. Dagon, was traveling in the following company. A horseman went after the doctor, but Sager refused to wait. Carefully he straightened Catherine's leg and prepared cloth and sticks to make a splint. By the time Henry had put the splint on the broken leg, Dr. Dagon came galloping up. He dismounted and knelt alongside Catherine. Then, turning to Henry, he said, "Vhy, Sir, it is chust as good as I do myself." He picked her up and carried her to the rear of the wagon to place Catherine inside next to her mother and baby sister. The wagons jolted on, and Dr. Dagon rode close to the Sagers.[46]

The wagons did not stop at the usual time that evening. Instead there was an increased pace, and an excitement in the air made men urge their tired oxen on into the dusk. Fort Laramie, the fur-trading post, came into view as the last lingering light flickered over the hills. Laramie was not a magnificent establishment, nor did it have many supplies to sell the emigrants. But it looked large, permanent, and important

Fort Laramie, 1846. While properly known as Fort John in the 1840's, emigrants called it Fort Laramie. (Watercolor by Paul Rockwood is at Scotts Bluff National Monument, Neb. Courtesy National Park Service.)

to these people who had not seen a structure of any kind for almost three months. In those early days on the Oregon Trail, it was the last American outpost of any importance. With the exception of the new but humbler Fort Bridger, all posts farther west were British.

The wagons passed the shadow of the fort and circled into camp two miles west, near the semi-permanent Sioux encampment. John and Francis were probably witnesses when a number of Sioux, waving five splendid banners, came into the camp to receive their blackmail — "presents" of tobacco, powder, and lead — and to smoke the traditional pipe.[47] Then sleep settled over the caravan, while outside the tents the murmur of sentinels and the ceaseless barking of innumerable Indian dogs marked the hours of the night.

Seven Orphans

Aware that snow would soon be falling on the Blue Mountains of Oregon, the emigrants stopped only two nights at Laramie. On August 1, the wagons lined up once again and headed west. Now the sun shone more often than it had back on the Kansas. Morning after morning, the brazen ball rose high in the sky, bleaching the blue to a hot white. The rich spring greens of the prairie had dried out and tans and browns covered the growing swells and gullies. But even now the days of rain made themselves remembered with grief. Here and there throughout the train, a child or a parent fell ill with a burning fever. For want of a better diagnosis, the pioneers called it "camp fever." On August 4, a Mrs. Susan Seabren died from it and was buried on the side of the trail. Eight days later, Mrs. Frost passed away. On August 15, a little daughter of John Nichols died.[48]

Passing the landmark of Independence Rock, the Great Register of the Desert, where many men had already written their names with tar or in painfully incised letters, the wagons stopped on the bank of the cool, clear Sweetwater. During this one day's camp, many of the travelers walked or rode the short distance to the Devil's Gap, a strange formation where the Sweetwater had cut a narrow, sheer-walled channel through a ridge of solid rock. Some of the more adventurous climbed to the top of the ridge and cautiously looked over the precipice at the foaming current directly below. Then, on August 23, the companies entered the broad South Pass and crossed that imperceptible line, the Continental Divide.[49] From now on the creeks and rivers flowed toward the Pacific. The old life of hard times and crowded land lay behind. Now it was all downhill, or so it seemed for the moment. The next evening, August 24, both Shaw's and Morrison's companies camped one-half mile from the Ford caravan, "and the hills and the valley became the scene of life and animation again for the evening."

"Near View of Devil's Gap" on the Sweetwater, from Osborne Cross report on plains crossing of Mounted Rifle Regiment, 1849. (*Sen. Ex. Doc. No. 1,* 31 Cong., 2 Sess.)

On August 26, the caravan reached the Green River near its junction with the Big Sandy. The Green was already famous, for along its banks the mountain men had many times gathered for their annual, free-swinging rendezvous at which Narcissa Whitman and Eliza Spalding, the missionaries' wives, were mobbed by Indian women in a wild scene of greeting in 1836. They had been the first white women to penetrate the Rockies. It had been only eight years since then, but times had already changed radically. The beaver industry had decreased greatly, and the mountain men had already left for the settlements of Oregon and Missouri. No more would the valleys echo to their wild, romantic free-for-alls each summer. The hills had grown quiet.

Things were strangely quiet around the Sager wagon this day also. Not only did Naomi and Catherine lie ill, now Henry himself had come down with camp fever. A few days before reaching the Green River, he had felt the illness coming on.

But his stubborn body had fought off the nausea, and Henry had declared himself well again. But the illness was still in him waiting to renew its attack. Then Henry made his error. "One day four buffalo ran between our wagon and the one behind. Father, though feeble, seized his gun and gave chase. This imprudent act again prostrated him and it soon became apparent to all that he must die."[50]

Young John Minto wrote in his diary for August 26, "At this camp I was again called upon for extra duty on account of the sick. About bedtime I was appealed to by Mrs. Shaw to sit up part of the night with Mr. Sager, who was very ill; and she said that Mrs. Sager was nearly down sick herself, but would see to giving her husband medicine; if I would watch in his tent and inform her at the time, to administer it."

Through the long night Minto woke Mrs. Sager when it was time to give Henry more medicine. Naomi would drag herself from her quilts to give her husband the medicine. "The sick man was either wholly or partly unconscious from high fever, and did not during the night ask for anything. On the two or three times I awakened her, his wife responded each time as though she was in fear that he was dead." No one came to relieve Minto. Until dawn he kept watch over the sick man, "suffering from inability to help this life, which seemed to be burning away."[51]

On the 28th the wagons crossed the Green River. Henry was carried over in his own wagon. As the men lifted him from his wagon to a tent, Henry gazed at his crippled Catherine and spoke softly, "Poor child, what will become of you?"[52] A few minutes later, William Shaw entered the tent and found Henry weeping. When Shaw tried to comfort him, Henry, his voice broken with helplessness, said he knew he was dying. He worried about his family — his ailing wife, his crippled daughter, the baby, and the rest of them. Pleadingly, he asked Captain Shaw to take care of the children and to take them to Marcus Whitman's mission station. Solemnly Shaw made his promise.[53] Within a short time, Henry Sager, aged 38, died. His plan for an earthly paradise died with him.

The simple funeral was held the next day. The body, placed in a coffin made of a split, hollowed-out log, was buried beside the swift stream.[54] When the wagons of 1845 reached this spot, the emigrants found Henry Sager's remains scattered about the ground. These travelers decided Indians had opened the grave to rob the body of its clothing. More likely, wild animals had disturbed the grave, just as they did many times throughout the West when graves were dug too shallow and not covered with stones. Nevertheless it was a sobering sight. One of the witnesses wrote it was a "reminder that we knew not when we would have to leave some of our loved ones to this same fate."[55]

As the caravan prepared to move on toward the Snake River, the Sagers presented a forlorn sight. Naomi, rapidly growing weaker, had scarcely the courage left to plan the next step. John and Francis, heartbroken over their father's death, were showing alarming symptoms of camp fever themselves. Although they were not to become seriously ill, the slightest sign of sickness sent terror through Naomi's mind. Catherine's shattered leg was healing but slowly. Elizabeth was old enough to know fear and discouragement. Although Matilda and Louise were too small to comprehend their plight, the baby suffered because of Naomi's sickness.

Dr. Dagon, firmly convinced the family needed his help, offered to drive the oxen. But Naomi did not fully trust the foreign doctor and turned to the men of the train for assistance. Unabashed, Dagon remained close to the wagon and helped when allowed to. A young man, still unattached, was hired to drive the Sagers on to Fort Bridger.[56]

A few days later Shaw's company arrived at the fort, situated on Black's Fork. It was a humble post and barely deserved the credit of being a trading center. Jim Bridger, growing tired of making history as a mountain man and interested now mainly in preserving legends, had established it just the year before. Had John and Francis known it and had they been interested, they could have met one of the more colorful mountain men, Kit Carson, who was at the fort. But even an adult, who had heard of him before and who now talked to him, did not know until later that it was the already-fabled Carson. Kit was spending most of these days scouting for Captain Frémont in his explorations of the far west for the United States Army.[57] John and Francis were probably unaware also that they were in

Mexican territory. This land had not yet been carefully surveyed and it is likely that most of the emigrants had no idea they had left the United States and were on foreign soil, if only for a few miles.[58]

Perhaps it is well that the name of the hired driver for the Sager wagon has not survived. No sooner had the wagons left Fort Bridger than he asked Mrs. Sager for the use of the only musket she had. He said he would ride out to hunt for game so that the children could have fresh meat. He took the gun, rode off, and was not seen again. Catherine learned later that he had gone on to a company ahead to tag on to the wagon of a young woman he was courting.[59] Whether or not she ever came face to face with him in later years she did not say.

Again, Dr. Dagon offered to drive the oxen. This time Naomi did not refuse. She no longer had the strength to doubt his offer. Catherine, still riding on the wagon bed with her mother, wrote that Naomi Sager planned to get to the Whitmans and winter there, but she was rapidly failing: "The nights and mornings were bitter cold; and the exposure to which she was necessarily subject produced a violent cold. But although consumed with fever and afflicted with a sore mouth that was the forerunner of the fatal camp fever, she refused to give up, but fought bravely against disease and weakness for the sake of her children." Naomi became delirious and "She talked continuously of her husband, at times addressing him as though present, and beseeching him in piteous tones to relieve her sufferings," until at last she became unconscious.[60]

On and on the wagons jolted, across the Big and Little Muddy Creeks, and over the Bear River Divide. The trail was much rougher here than it had been on the plains. Mrs. Sager, in a moment of consciousness, said to Elizabeth, "Now I know why your father begged to be taken out of the wagon when he was sick — it seems as if it would be easier to die than to stand any more of this jolting."[61]

The stop at Fort Hall, the most eastern of the Hudson's Bay posts in the Oregon Country, made no great impression on the Sager children. Perhaps John noticed the factor, Captain Richard "Johnny" Grant, an honest man who thought the emigrants would make better time if they abandoned their

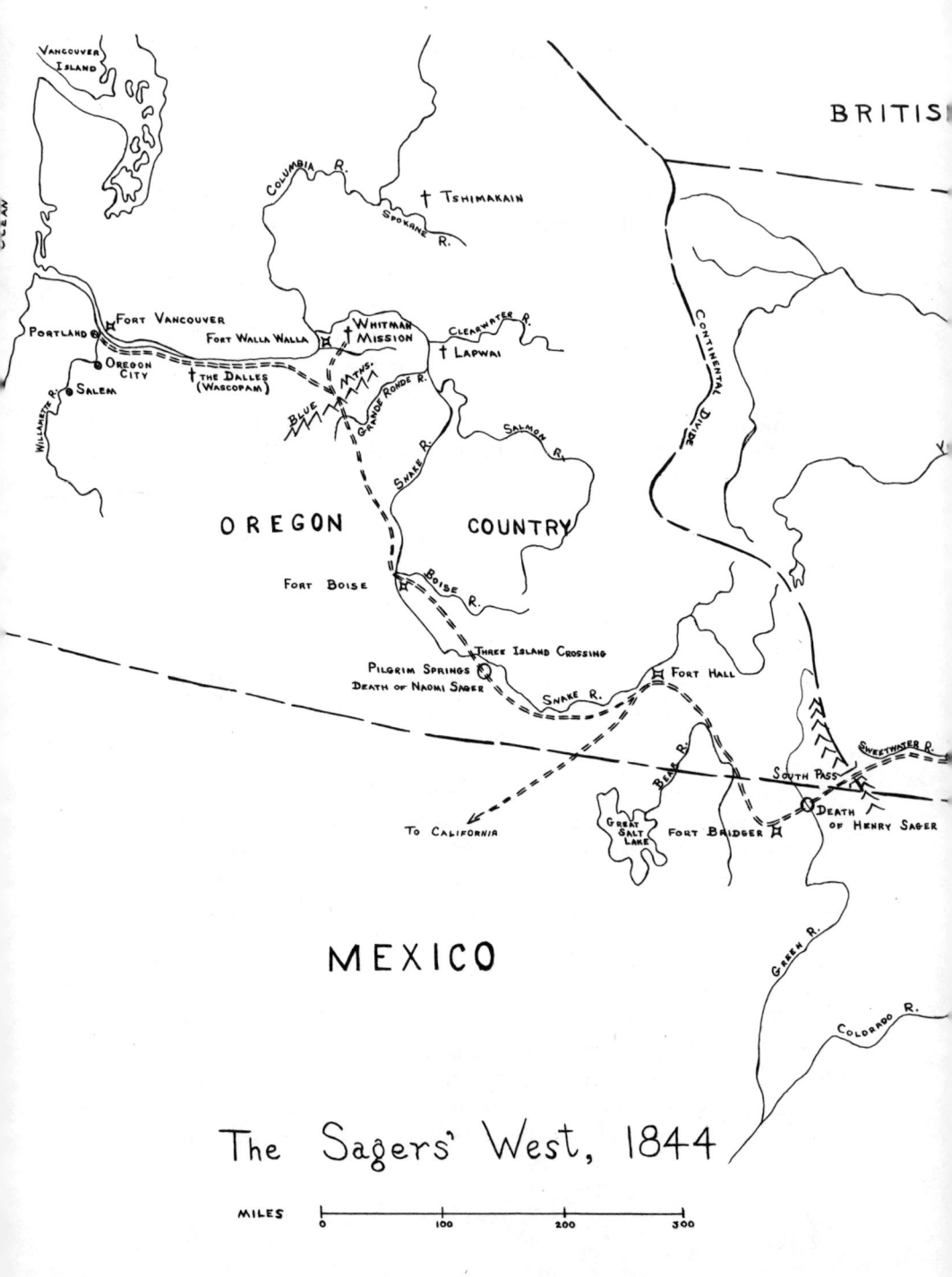

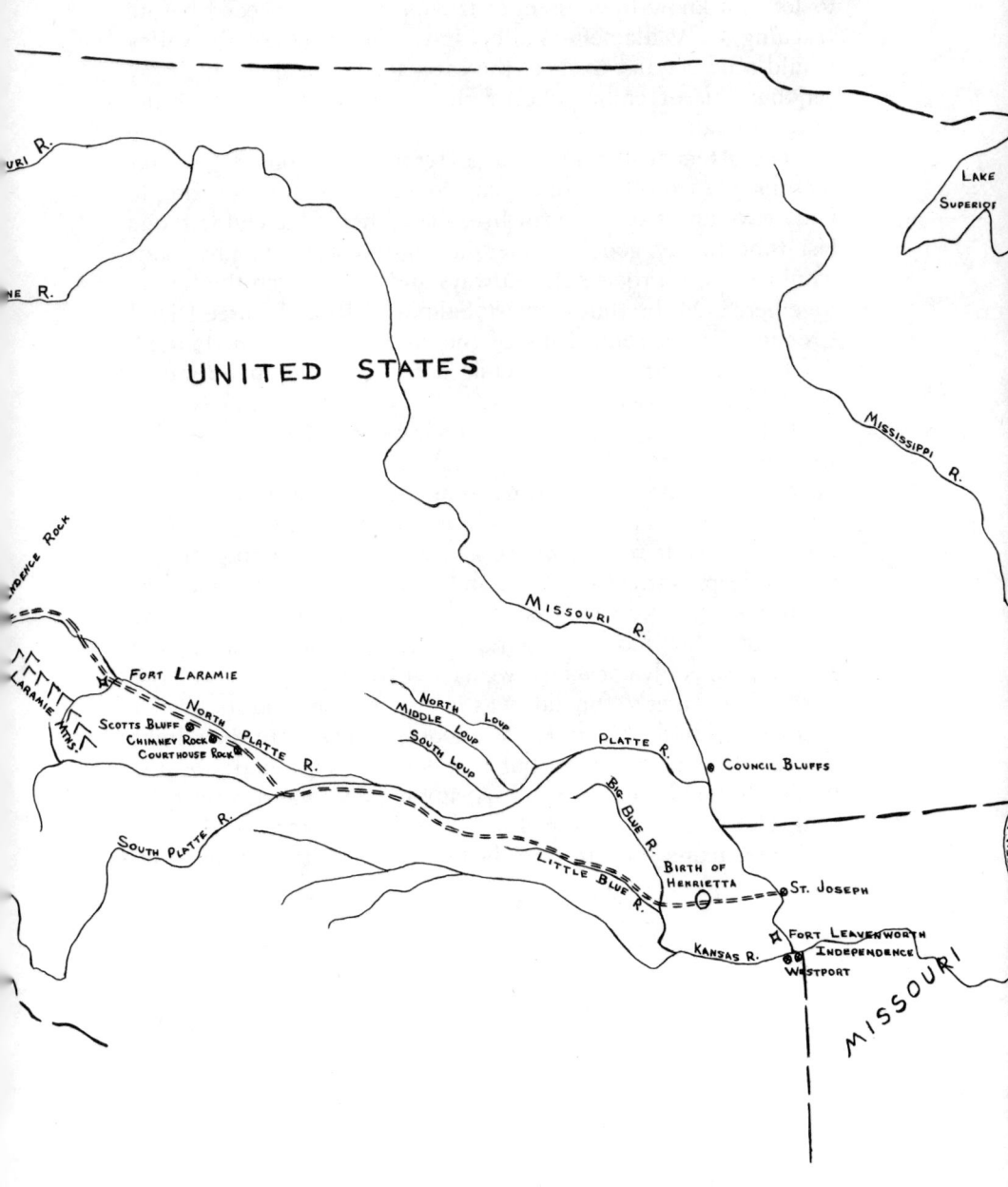

wagons. But the Americans did not heed his advice; their wagons would go all the way. Captain Grant handed William Shaw a letter from Peter H. Burnett, an old friend who had emigrated the year before. In his note, Burnett urged Shaw to let him know by messenger if supplies were needed before reaching the Willamette Valley. If so, the people of the valley would send a relief to meet the caravan. It was not a highway yet, but this offer bespoke of the rapid development of the Oregon Trail.

The offers of help made no difference to Naomi Sager. Her months of suffering were coming to an end. Before her fragile body gave up its struggle for life, she gathered her children one last time to say goodbye. Her last hopes were that her sons would stay with their sisters always and would keep the family together.[62] On the trail between Salmon Falls and Three Island Crossing, on the south bank of the Snake, Naomi quietly died. She was buried at a place the emigrants called Pilgrim Springs.[63] Her pilgrimage was finally over.

Catherine wrote of her mother's last day, "The day she died we traveled over a very rough road. . . . When we camped at night, one of the women came in as usual to wash her. To her inquiry if she wished her face washed, she made no reply as she had done at former times, and the woman, supposing her to be asleep, washed her face, and then taking up her hand to cleanse it, she discovered that the pulse was nearly gone. . . . She lived but a few moments more, and her last words were, 'Oh Henry, if you only knew how we have suffered.' "[64]

Naomi Sager's funeral was as simple as had been her husband's. Elizabeth wrote, "We looked everywhere for a light colored dress of mother's, but it was not to be found; we had to bury her in a calico dress."[65] A simple grave was dug near the trail. Her body was wrapped in a bed sheet. A few words were said. Her name was cut on a headboard. The train moved on.

"Your Children Have Come"

The families of the caravan, particularly those who had been good friends of Henry and Naomi, wasted little time in planning the care of the seven orphans. Dr. Dagon continued his role as driver and anxiously watched over the children. His chief assistant was quiet, intense John who, remembering his mother's request not to let the family be divided, suddenly found himself grown up. There was no time for mourning. He hid his hurt and attempted to govern and care for his brother and sisters.

An immediate problem was the baby. Barely four months old and very ill, she needed a woman's care. For the next few weeks the baby would be passed from mother to mother, and it would share with their own babies these women's breasts. This arrangement was not organized enough to be called a system, but it worked.[66] The Sager baby would reach the Whitman mission alive.

For the rest of the journey the two boys and their other four sisters, Catherine, Elizabeth, Louise, and Matilda, traveled together, although "literally adopted by the train."[67] The Shaws and the other families in the company shared their dwindling food supplies with the orphans and the doctor. In future years the girls were to write repeatedly, "We were all taken care of by the company. There was not one but would share their bread with us."[68] Miles Cannon, who later interviewed the Sager survivors extensively, mentions that Mrs. Shaw, Mrs. John Nichols, and a Mrs. Daniels "were constant visitors to the Sager camp." Another woman who helped by nursing the baby was Mrs. Eads, the mother of the young man who had been "bound over for good behavior" months ago on the plains.[69]

The first bright days of spring now lay far behind. The call, "Catch up," was becoming tinged with urgency. Over the horizon the Blue Mountains waited, teasing, cajoling. Would they lie dark and naked until the wagons crossed? Or would

Three Islands Crossing of the Snake River. Oregon Trail crossed the further two islands, from about central right (south), to central left (north). View is upstream (east). (Courtesy Merle Wells, Idaho State Historical Society.)

they twist the tail of fate and hug the first of the winter storms close to their black plateaus before the wagons arrived?

Just as the Sager wagon was crossing the ford at Three Islands between the pale yellow banks of the Snake, it collapsed from its months of burden. Undoubtedly, there was talk of splitting up the children among the families and abandoning the wagon. The Sagers' flour was gone, and the Whitmans' mission was still a month away. But if these thoughts were voiced, another counsel prevailed. The men quickly converted the wagon into a cart by chopping off the rear half. The remaining goods were repacked and the weary oxen were yoked to this lighter burden. Dagon cracked his frayed whip as best he knew and the chains again creaked under the strain. The children moved on, still together, and Captain Shaw kept his promise to the dead.

Still, the adults worried, and at times the Sager children did too. But youth does not know how to hold on to its hurt. There were times of remembering and tears, but there were growing times too when the Sagers laughed. It was Elizabeth who recalled the terrible temper of Dr. Dagon which would explode when the oxen were stubborn. Never would he admit his ignorance of how to handle the beasts. But he would delightfully shock the girls with his English-German curses. In reprimand, Elizabeth is said to have once slipped up behind him when he was cursing, and planted a dainty kick on the doctor's rear. Giggling, she dodged back to the shelter of her sisters. Catherine recalled another incident when her brothers had loaded the back end of the cart with pieces from a freshly-killed beef. Later, Dagon, paying no heed to this new load, piled the bedding and utensils on the cart as he had on other mornings, "When he got so much back of the center of gravity as to tip the cart up, whereupon he set up a hallooing and scrambling that was very amusing to lookers-on."[70]

The companies lumbered through the endless sage, away from the eroded gut of the Snake River, toward the Boise. The younger single men could almost smell the ocean and they grew increasingly restless. With a few days' rations tied to their saddles, many of them left the wagon train on a final dash to the Columbia. The strains of forced companionship showed in the family groups too. Companies splintered; a few wagons would start a little earlier one morning, and the campfires would be a little farther apart that evening. But the core of the Shaw company remained united, and the Sagers were a part of this.

Catherine wrote of those days, "There was not one in it but was ready to do us a favor. But most especially this was the case with Captain Shaw and his wife. Their kindness will ever be cherished with grateful remembrance by us. Our parents would not have been more solicitous or careful for us." She added, "To this day Uncle Billy and Aunt Sally, as we familiarly call them, regard us with the affection of parents."[71]

Crossing the Snake for the last time near the Hudson's Bay Company's Fort Boise, Shaw's company reached Farewell Bend, then moved through the narrow valley of the Burnt River.[72]

1849 views of Snake River sagebrush plains, and of Fort Boise, near junction of Boise and Snake rivers. The Sagers were orphans when they reached this fur trading post. (*Sen. Ex. Doc. No. 1*, 31 Cong., 2 Sess.)

Within this precipitous canyon the trail gave up seeking a hold on the slope and dropped into the rocky course of the river itself. Climbing the brown hills, the train came to the Powder River, then dropped into the beautiful valley some unknown fur trapper had named the Grande Ronde. This peaceful valley of deep grasses, watered by a crystal-clear stream, was the delight of every trapper, trader, and emigrant who came this way. But the delight was tempered this autumn by the dark mass of the Blue Mountains that filled the sky on the western rim of the valley. There was no easy pass through these pine-packed hills. The trail twisted up and over the boulder-strewn sides to the broad plateaus on top. It was considered to be the most difficult part of the Oregon Trail.

As the first evening in the valley came on, the crisp cold fingers of autumn worked their way down the draws and the people moved closer to their fires. Louise Sager stepped up to the blazing wood to capture its heat. A flame flickered, disappeared momentarily, then reappeared at the hem of her dress. She screamed. Dr. Dagon grabbed her and beat out the fire. His hands were burnt, but he had saved the child from serious injury, if not death.[73] The incident was a reminder that the emigrants were still in the grasp of a fierce environment. Although the Whitman mission lay just beyond the range, there could be no relaxing yet.

It took several days for Captain Shaw's group to cross the mountains. The past months of strain on the wagons and the oxen became very apparent, both in pulling the wagons up the steep slopes and again when lowering them on the western side.[74] In both cases it was necessary to hitch several teams to one wagon at a time. The first snows were already falling as this company crossed the Blues. Later wagons that year were caught in near blizzards.

These were wet and miserably cold days. As if fate were administering the final tests of endurance to the orphans, two more incidents occurred on the mountains. One night, Captain Shaw was awakened by the cries of a child. He went outside his tent to find that one of the younger Sager girls had got out of her shelter and was wandering, lost and close to freezing.[75] Then, at one of the last mountain camps, Francis helped Dr.

Dagon to start a campfire. The two were having trouble getting the wet wood to burn. Francis decided to fix the situation by sprinkling a little gunpowder on the fretful flames. The powder horn exploded in his hands. Some instinct caused him to run to the nearby brook where he threw water on his face and hands. He returned to the fire without his eyelashes and brows, and his face was thoroughly blackened. But it proved not to be a serious incident. In retrospect, the children could see the event as a rather funny sight.[76]

Descending the Blue Mountains, the wagons traveled down the Umatilla River, going into camp near the present town of Pendleton. This was Cayuse country, the Indians among whom Dr. Whitman had established his mission. The emigrants had already met a few Cayuses as far east as the Grande Ronde and had found them to be different from the Indians of the eastern plains. With Whitman's encouragement, many of the Cayuses had planted small fields of wheat and potatoes, and had established the beginning of cattle herds. They were anxious to sell or trade these crops and beef to the emigrants.[77] Whitman hoped these modest beginnings at ranching and farming would encourage the Indians to give up their semi-nomadic way of life and to settle in permanent communities. He was convinced that only by this means could he prepare them for the inevitable advance of civilization that was going to overtake them.

The emigrants to Oregon reacted many different ways to the Cayuses upon their first encounters. All of them, true to their own traditions, tried their best to outwit the Indians at trading. Those who succeeded in driving hard bargains tended to describe the Cayuses in friendly if condescending terms. Those whites who were worsted, which case was not rare, generally reacted with bitterness and considered the Indians to be treacherous and unworthy people.

The Umatilla camp was the parting place for those going directly westward to the Willamette Valley and for those detouring by way of the Whitman mission, 40 miles to the north. Until this year, all emigrants had ridden to the mission. But a thousand or more people pouring down on the small station was more than it could ably handle; also, in going to the mission the emigrants lost four or five days of valuable

Descending the Blue Mountains toward the Umatilla. Here the Sagers were in Cayuse country, only 40 miles from their new home, Whitman mission. (*Sen. Ex. Doc. No. 1,* 31 Cong., 2 Sess.)

time because of the added distance. The Willamette Valley was still 200 miles away.

Because of this, Marcus Whitman and some of the earlier emigrants had already marked the shorter trail bypassing the mission, in order to encourage the newcomers to travel directly down the Umatilla to the Columbia. From 1844 on, only the destitute, the sick, and the tired made the detour to Waiilatpu. Even so, these unfortunates generally amounted to significant numbers. Narcissa Whitman accurately described this role of the station in an 1844 letter, "Here we are, one family alone, a way mark, as it were, or center post, about which multitudes will or must gather this winter. And these we must feed and warm to the extent of our powers."

Captain Shaw left the Sagers with his family at the Umatilla camp and rode on horseback to the mission to talk to Marcus and Narcissa Whitman about accepting the children. From earlier travelers that autumn, the Whitmans had already heard about the children, but had not yet decided what they could or should do about them. Narcissa had written on October 9: "It

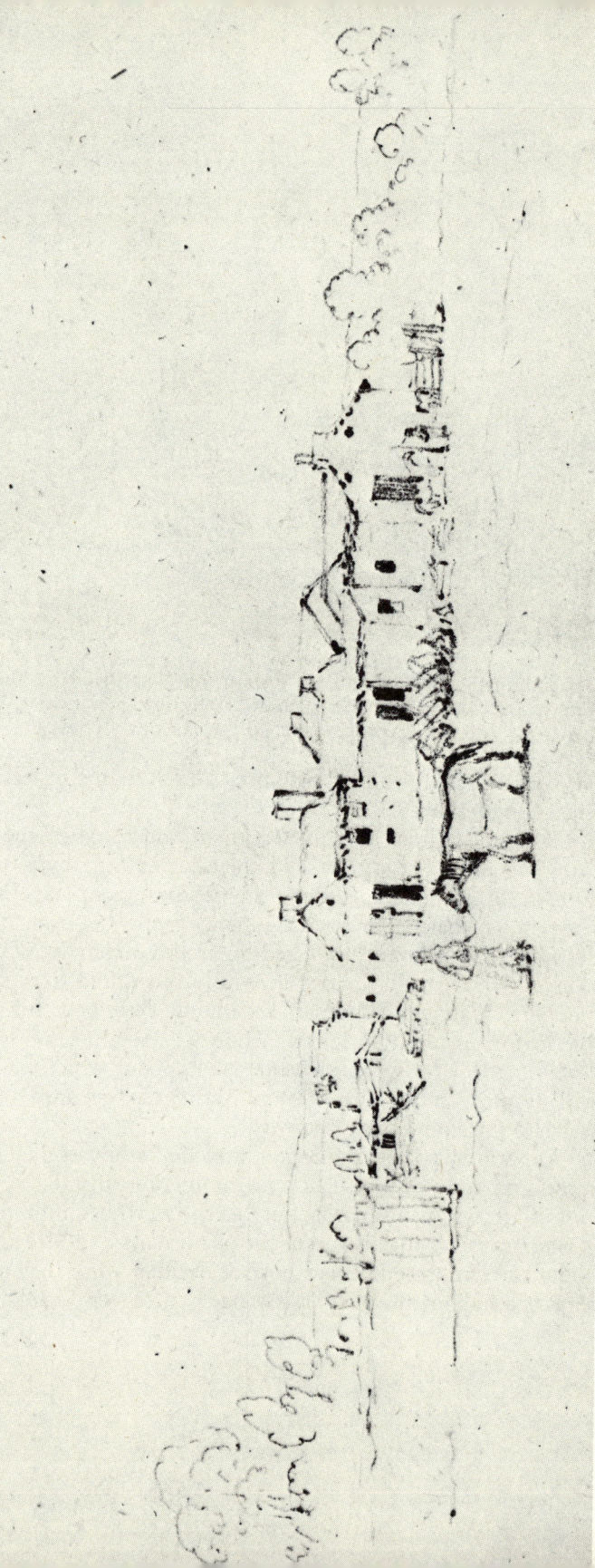

The Whitmans' mission at Waiilatpu, sketch in 1847 by Paul Kane. This is the only known sketch of the mission made before its destruction. The girl with the broom at right may be one of the Sagers. (Courtesy Royal Ontario Museum, Toronto, Canada.)

is expected there are more than five hundred souls back in the snow and mountains. Among the number is an orphan family of seven children, the youngest infant born on the way, whose parents have both died since they left the States. Application has been made for us to take them, as they have not a relative in the company. What we shall do I cannot say; we cannot see them suffer, if the Lord casts them upon us."[78]

No account of Shaw's first interview with the Whitmans has been found. However, within three days he was back at the Umatilla camp where he told the children they were going to stay with the missionaries, for a while at least. Catherine recalled: "on the morning of the 17th [October] we started for our destination." She recalled that "The Captain's wife took affectionate leave of us and stood looking after us as long as we were in sight."[79] Elizabeth's memory of the scene was similar: "Aunt Sally washed us and put on our best dresses. I can remember yet how the tears ran down her face as she said, 'I wonder what fate has in store for you little orphan children.' "[80]

When the small group approached the mission establishment, Shaw spurred his horse and rode ahead. On reaching the white, adobe mission house, he dismounted and entered. Narcissa Whitman received him in the kitchen where she was busy with her chores. A few minutes later, Shaw glanced through the window and saw Dr. Dagon bring the cart up to the irrigation ditch just a few yards away. As Dagon unyoked the oxen, Shaw said to Mrs. Whitman, "Your children have come; will you go out and see them?" He preceded her out the doorway and told John and Francis to help their sisters out of the cart and to find their bonnets. But Narcissa was right behind him and the children were still searching madly for their bonnets when they became aware of her. All movement ceased.

A tableau was caught in time and space. A little way off from the cart Narcissa Whitman stood, calm and serene on the outside but worried and concerned within. Near her an Indian woman sat on the ground, passively observing the drama. William Shaw stood near Narcissa watching her and the children. Off to one side, near the oxen, stood Dr. Dagon. He was fighting, vainly, to hold back his tears. His job was at an end, for he brought his six charges safely to this strange place. Catherine would never forget the moment: "sitting in the front end of the cart was John weeping bitterly. On the opposite side stood Francis with his arm on the wheels and his head resting on them, sobbing aloud. On the near side stood the little girls huddled together, bare-headed and bare-footed, looking first at the boys and then at the house, dreading we knew not what."

When Narcissa, dressed in dark calico and a gingham sunbonnet, broke the spell and smiled, "we thought . . . she was the prettiest woman we had ever seen." She directed Dagon and the two boys where to carry the few possessions from the cart. Then, seeing that Catherine was lame, Narcissa took her by the arm and led her toward the house. The rest followed. Captain Shaw, perhaps noticing the Indian features of Helen Mar Meek, one of the mission children, asked Mrs. Whitman if she had any children of her own. Pausing for a moment, a shadow of sadness flickering across her face, Narcissa pointed to the mission cemetery at the foot of the nearby hill. Softly she answered, "All the child I ever had sleeps yonder."[81] The death by drowning five years earlier of the Whitmans' only child, Alice Clarissa, the first child born of American parents in the Pacific Northwest, was still a great hurt in the mission household.

Dr. Whitman came to the house and stood in the doorway. A slight expression of surprise moved over his face. Catherine thought that he had cause to be surprised: "dirty and sunburnt until we looked more like Indians than white children. Added to this, John had cropped our hair, so that it hung in uneven locks and added to our uncouth appearance." Marcus recovered and tried to welcome the children by picking up Louise. But she screamed and ran to Catherine, leaving the doctor feeling more uncomfortable than before.[82]

John and Francis told the doctor they wanted to go on to the Willamette. As soon as John was old enough to hold a land claim, he would send for his sisters. Although the Whitmans had not yet decided what to do about the seven children, Marcus persuaded the boys not to leave their sisters just then. He did not hesitate to use a subtle threat that he would not consider taking the girls unless their brothers stayed at the mission.[83]

The Whitmans were faced with a most difficult decision.

There were many good reasons for not taking the Sagers. For the past few years Narcissa's health had been very poor. In the preceding year, even her husband was certain she had only a short time to live. Although she had recovered some since then, she already had more than enough to do. There were four children in the household. Seven more seemed almost too many.[84]

Marcus was concerned too about the reaction of his missionary board in Boston. His purpose in Oregon was to act as a medical missionary to the Indians. He did not wish to become wholly diverted into the role of colonizer as had the Methodist missionaries in the Willamette. Already he had been reprimanded by the board for his assistance to the immigrant trains. However, Marcus knew that the caravans' stopping at Waiilatpu was inevitable and that he could not cease helping even if he wished.

In the end it came to this. The Whitmans would take the children. John and Francis would be sent up to Tshimakain to help Walker and Eells, while the Whitmans would keep the five girls. If Walker and Eells should decide they did not want the boys, then Whitman was free either to keep them or to send all seven down to the Willamette in the spring. Meanwhile, Narcissa knew she wanted the baby—that had not yet arrived. She expressed it this way: "Husband thought we could get along with all but the baby—he did not see how we could take that; but I felt that if I must take any, I wanted her as a charm to bind the rest to me."[85] They took all seven.

Waiilatpu Station Nov. 6, 1844

AGREEMENT between Wm Shaw and Dr. Marcus Whitman for the Sager family. Drawn [later] by C. Saxton, Esq., of Oregon City.

Be it known by these presents that I, Wm Shaw of Missourie on the way to the Oregon Territory, took charge of the orphan children of Mr. Henry Sager who died on the road and his widow soon after leaving seven orphan children: two boys, John C. and Francisco, the oldest 13 years of age and the other twelve, and five girls all younger than the boys, named Catherine, Elizabeth M., Matilda J., Hannah L., and Rosanna L. [Henrietta], which seven children I leave, together with the property of the deceased, consisting of three yoke of oxen, one waggon, one cow and one odd steer and several articles of clothing with Dr. Marcus Whitman at the Waiilatpu Station under the American Board of Missions in Oregon with the understanding that said

Whitman sends the two boys to Tshimakain Mission Station under the charge of Mr. Walker and Eells and this instrument further showeth that in case the said Walker and Eells do not wish to take the boys said Whitman is at liberty to keep and dispose of the seven or send them all down to me at Oregon City in the spring when I will again take charge of them until there [*sic*] case can be acted upon and places provided for them by the Oregon Court of Probate or charitable persons

Marcus Whitman
William Shaw.

In the presence of
James Cave
William Seling.

In the next summer, Whitman brought the document up to date:

One old cow, blind in one eye, recovered from the Indians at five and a half dollars expense.

Marcus Whitman
Oregon City, June 22, 1845.[86]

When Shaw had brought the children to Waiilatpu, the baby was still several days behind in the Perkins wagon. By the time the baby had reached the Umatilla, it had been transferred to the care of Mrs. Eads. The Eads wagon came to the mission and the dirty little bundle was handed to Narcissa Whitman who wrote, "she arrived here in the hands of an old filthy woman, sick, emaciated and but just alive." Continuing, Narcissa recounted, "She was five months old and when she was brought here—had suffered for the want of proper nourishment until she was nearly starved. The old woman did the best she could, but she was in distressed circumstances herself, and a wicked, disobedient family around her to see to."[87] In another letter Narcissa wrote, "You will be astonished to know that we have eleven children in our family, and not one of them our own by birth, but so it is." She added, "We must take them or they must perish."[88]

Seven months and 2,000 miles, both parents dead, the seven Sagers had finally reached Oregon. The fear and the pain of the journey now lay behind. As the days and weeks passed at Waiilatpu, the children were to find the security they needed. And they were to learn about the mission and the people whose house was now their home—Marcus and Narcissa Whitman.

Whitman Mission[89]

Marcus Whitman's quick interest in the two boys may have resulted from memories of his own youth. By the time he was 10, he too had been fatherless and was living with an uncle in upstate New York. That was still a frontier land when Marcus was born in Rushville in 1802.

His uncle made it possible for Marcus to attend classical school. Later, when he decided to become a minister, his family showed a complete lack of interest, even disdain, for the calling. Marcus succumbed to this disinterest and to a lack of money and decided to pursue a less expensive course by becoming a doctor. For a while he rode with the local doctor then, in 1825, entered the medical school at Fairfield, New York. Following this brief encounter with the classroom, he practiced for the next few years in several localities including a village in Ontario, Canada. Then he settled in Wheeler, New York.

Physically well-built, but bothered with vague sickness from time to time, the sandy-haired doctor entered his 30's still a bachelor. His deep interest in religion remained with him and he gave increasing thought to the idea of combining his interest and his profession by becoming a medical missionary. In the 1830's, a great revival spread throughout the United States; one of the results of this movement was a rapid expansion in the foreign mission field by all the established churches. Whitman, a Presbyterian, was further influenced by this movement and, finally, offered himself to the American Board of Commissioners for Foreign Missions, which was supported by the Presbyterian, Congregational, and Dutch Reformed churches. But the Board reviewed Whitman's background and turned him down because of his history of illness.

Then another door opened to Whitman's ambitions. In 1835, the eccentric, egotistical Samuel Parker, just recently appointed by (or forced upon) the American Board as a missionary to the Indians of the Far West, interviewed Whitman as a potential assistant. Parker recommended that the Board reconsider and appoint Whitman. The Board did so, and Marcus prepared to travel west that spring. It would be appropriate to say that Whitman and Parker made one of the most unusual teams ever to head west—except that the American Board, without much choice in the matter, followed them up with even more unlikely combinations. The autocratic, cantankerous Parker insisted on treating Whitman as his personal servant. Whitman, stubborn to a fault, performed his menial labors silently but was embarrassed. He reserved his hurt for a later time when, in a rare outburst, he would write the American Board and scald Parker in a kettle of criticism.

Their first good row occurred in Liberty, Missouri, when Parker insisted that all their supplies could be carried on one mule. Whitman insisted that not only was this impossible but the purchase of a second animal would in the long run prove more economical. But penny-pinching Parker was adamant; there would be but one mule and, furthermore, Whitman would pack it. It was Whitman's misfortune that he attempted to pack the animal in front of some of the continent's best packers and mountain men who were lounging about in the frontier village. They watched in amazement at the doctor's procedures. Everything he did was wrong. As a final climax, no sooner had Whitman and his off-balance mule started down the street, when the whole load rolled off the animal's back and fell with a clattering smash on the road. A few pots and pans stuck to the poor animal's belly, and it and Marcus panicked together.[90]

The two missionaries traveled westward with the annual fur trade caravan which was heading for the rendezvous with the trappers, to be held that year near the junction of Horse Creek and the Green River. The hardened traders did not welcome the missionaries in their midst and subjected them to derision and name-calling. But when cholera hit the train and Whitman was able to contain it, he gained a certain amount of respect for himself and Parker. Later, at the rendezvous, he favorably impressed both mountain men and the Indians by skillfully removing a stubborn iron arrowhead that had been hooked into one of Jim Bridger's vertebrae for the past several years.

At the rendezvous, the missionaries met and talked with Nez Percé and Flathead Indians from the area that is now central Idaho and western Montana. These tribes had been willing for some years to have missions in their homelands, not so much because they wanted Christianity but because they believed the missionaries could teach them the secrets of white man's inventions and power. Just the year before, Jason Lee, a Methodist, had established a mission among the Willamette Valley Indians of the Pacific Northwest. Now the Nez Percés persuaded Parker and Whitman that they would be most welcome to dwell among the tribe.

To save a year's time, Parker proposed that he go on to the Oregon Country, explore the Nez Percé lands, and select sites for mission stations. He directed Whitman to hasten home to recruit workers and to meet him next spring at the rendezvous. Marcus was a little worried about Parker's riding off without him. He need not have been. Parker spent the winter in virtual luxury, exploring the country in good weather, eating off the ironstone dinnerware of the Hudson's Bay Company posts during the snows. It would be of little comfort to Whitman to learn later that Parker treated the mighty Hudson's Bay Company's factors as haughtily as ever he did Marcus.

The doctor had another reason besides recruiting to cause him to hurry home. Just before he had left New York, he had met and proposed to an attractive young spinster, Narcissa Prentiss, who lived in Prattsburg. Endowed with a fine figure, a good face, and an excellent voice, it is a wonder that this 27-year-old woman had not long since married some stalwart upstater. That she had not was probably due to her strict puritanical approach to life. Underneath her considerable vivaciousness and ready wit lay a sharp mind that questioned all people and all things in terms of her own stern religious convictions. Marcus Whitman met all these tests.

Like him, she had applied to the American Board for a foreign mission. She too had been turned down. In her case, it was a matter of her sex. The Board was not yet willing to undertake sending single women to the distant corners of the world. Their meeting was probably an arranged one, since mutual friends could easily have foreseen a sensible marriage.

Although their engagement was a long one, because of Marcus' trip west with Parker, they actually knew little about each other on their wedding day, February 18, 1836. But the alchemy of similar interests worked for them. Their marriage was quickly reinforced with romantic love as well as with mutual understanding and admiration.

It was a strange little group that set out from Liberty, Missouri, in April 1836, hastening to catch up with the fur traders' caravan. Besides the newly-weds there were the Reverend Henry and Eliza Spalding and William H. Gray.

Spalding had been enlisted as the ordained minister of the group; Gray had been recruited as a mechanic and carpenter. The American Board had not been very enthusiastic about selecting the Spaldings, who had already agreed to be missionaries on the Great Plains. Neither was Whitman overjoyed. But there was no one else available and no time left for further searching. Marcus may not have known Henry Spalding before this spring, but Narcissa had. Henry had attended Franklin Academy the same time as she. The dour little fanatic had either fallen in love with her or thought she would make a good partner in the religious life and had futilely proposed marriage—or so Narcissa's sister was to say many years later.

Whether it was this proposal and its prompt rejection or some other relationship, feelings between Narcissa and Henry were greatly strained. So much so, that Narcissa's father thought it advisable to have a conference with Henry prior to his daughter's departure for Oregon. At this meeting Henry gave his promise not to bring up the past nor to criticize Narcissa's character. He soon broke his promise and the Whitmans and the Spaldings were to have many disagreements because of this in the months ahead.

Spalding had been born illegitimately in Bath, New York, in 1803. When less than two, he was turned over to foster parents who raised him, after a fashion. His foster father took to calling Henry "Bastard" and similar names. The uncertain, hurt boy grew into an embittered, suspicious, quick-tempered man. From Franklin Academy he had gone on to other schools, including Lane Theological Seminary in Cincinnati. In 1831, he married Eliza Hart, also from New York, but who had been

Later studio portrait photo of W. H. Gray. (OHS Collections.)

born in Kensington, Connecticut. She was many of the things Henry was not: patient, reserved, shy, but charming. It is said she was not pretty but had good manners and a sense of humanity that ran much deeper than looks.

Born in Fairfield, New York, in 1810, William Gray was apprenticed to a cabinetmaker when 16. Although he had become a good carpenter, he was an ambitious man who continually sought a higher plane in life than whatever he was doing at the moment. He was employed by the Board as a mechanic and carpenter, important jobs in the isolation of the Nez Percé country. But Gray's desperate desire to be a full-fledged missionary in his own right was to cause Marcus Whitman and his associates many a worried thought in the next few years. These five headed west.

The most significant accomplishment of that 1836 journey was its successful completion by Eliza and Narcissa. They were the first white women, perhaps the first women, ever to cross America, almost from shore to shore. This successful journey, across the Great American Desert, the fabled Rocky Mountains, and stretches of virtually unknown land—as far as the average American was concerned—had a singular impact on those who were then being stirred to think about Oregon. These two proved that women could successfully do it. The Oregon Trail (a term not yet in use) thus took a long step toward reality, and the waiting people such as Henry and Naomi Sager could now consider such a journey with a little more cause for hope.

The travelers celebrated July 4 that year by going through South Pass, thus crossing the Continental Divide. Two days later, they arrived at the rendezvous on the Green River, near Daniel, Wyoming. Narcissa and Eliza were the stars of the wild, tumultuous affair. Never before had their likes been seen that far west. Indian and trapper got as close as they dared to gaze upon them. Eliza withdrew from the limelight and concentrated on preparing herself for the role of missionary. Already she had begun the arduous task of learning the complicated Nez Percé language. Not so Narcissa; she glowed in the glances of admiration, and enjoyed the excitement, though careful not to condone the sinning she saw about her.

There was one disappointment when Parker did not appear at the rendezvous as he had planned. Instead, he sent a letter or two mentioning briefly what he had seen, recommending that a mission be established among the Nez Percés or among their neighbors, the Cayuses. But his recommendations lacked detail and were not of great value. Where was Parker? He was on his way home by sea. He had given up the missionary life. It might have been that Parker was feeling his age—he was in his late fifties. Or it might have been that he saw a ready market back home for a good book describing the Oregon

Country. At any rate, he promptly wrote such a book on his return, and it proved to be popular.

From the rendezvous the missionaries rode on toward their destination guided by the traders of the Hudson's Bay Company. Despite a good deal of difficulty with Henry Spalding's light wagon, which they soon reduced to a cart, the missionaries got the thing as far west as Fort Boise on the Snake River. This was but a few hundred miles short of the Columbia and, along with the journey of the women, this accomplishment was another landmark in the history of the Oregon Trail. No wheeled vehicle had come this far west before.

From Fort Boise, the trail crossed over increasingly rugged country, climaxing with the Blue Mountains. Beyond that barrier the travelers were hospitably received by the Hudson's Bay factor, Pierre Pambrun, at Fort Walla Walla on the Columbia. On September 12, the party arrived at Fort Vancouver, the headquarters for the Hudson's Bay Company in the Oregon Country, and was met by the majestic Chief Factor, Dr. John McLoughlin. The journey had taken 207 days and had covered more than 3,000 miles, but Narcissa Whitman and Eliza Spalding arrived at Fort Vancouver in perfect fit and high spirits. Moreover, Narcissa was three months' pregnant.

While the women remained at Fort Vancouver to enjoy its civilized aspects, Whitman and Spalding traveled back up the Columbia to look for mission sites. Riding east from Fort Walla Walla they explored the Walla Walla Valley and decided that a particularly fertile piece of land, lying in the triangle between the Walla Walla River and one of its tributaries, was a likely looking place for a station for Whitman. (The two men had agreed already, it seems, that the mission would succeed the better if their personalities were separated by a few miles.) This was Waiilatpu, "Place of the Rye Grass," named by the Cayuses for a beautiful tall grass that is highly decorative but unsatisfactory as fodder, being too tough and sharp. Waiilatpu was 20 miles upstream from Fort Walla Walla, and in its vicinity a band of Cayuse Indians had built its lodges since time immemorial.

Moving eastward another 100 miles, the men found a principal Nez Percé village on Lapwai Creek just a few miles from its junction with the Clearwater, the beautiful river down which

Old Lapwai mission building at right, with Indians, canoe and circa 1890s home. (OHS Collections.)

Lewis and Clark had come to the Snake just 31 years earlier. The Nez Percés now got their long-awaited missionary, for Spalding decided he would establish his station here at Lapwai, "Butterfly Valley."

Narcissa came up the Columbia in December and joined her husband in their new home. She did not find much of a house—a crude log lean-to, barely a shelter against the oncoming winter. This shed had two tiny bedrooms, a kitchen, a pantry, and a fireplace, and it was still awaiting doors and windows. Even before the lean-to was completed, Whitman and his help worked to finish the house proper, a one-story adobe building with a mud roof to which the lean-to was attached.

The first two years at Waiilatpu were pleasant enough. Gaining the confidence of the proud Cayuses promised to be a job by itself. But Marcus had come here for this very purpose and he pursued their friendship with energy. Narcissa was happy in this new life too. To be sure, she had not yet got used to Indian men walking into her kitchen unannounced and sitting on the floor until fed. But the birth of her baby, Alice Clarissa, in March 1837, proved to be the blessing expected. Alice's parents gave her boundless love, and her arrival cemented her parents' relations with the Indians. One of the elderly leaders, who had picked up the concept of private property, decided that when he died Alice Clarissa should inherit all his real estate. The Indians called her *temi,* Cayuse girl, because she was born on their lands.

The Whitmans' nearest white neighbor was Pierre Pambrun at Fort Walla Walla. Although he represented the power of the Hudson's Bay Company in the area, and it was a company policy to discourage Americans from settling nearby, Pambrun recognized his obligations as a neighbor in the lonely wilderness. When Narcissa was still pregnant, he brought her a rocking chair and a small heating stove. Later, Marcus was able to treat the various illnesses of the Pambrun family in return for the favors.[91]

But there were many other visitors too in these early years before mass emigration on the Oregon Trail became a fact. Other Hudson's Bay traders, American mountain men, an occasional officer from either British or American forces, besides the trickle of emigrants already passing by, all stopped to enjoy the hospitality of the Whitmans.

Although he had the part-time assistance of William Gray and of one or two Hawaiian laborers borrowed from the Hudson's Bay Company, Whitman employed those able-bodied newcomers whom he could persuade to stay over for a season or so at the mission. There was lumber to be whipsawed in the Blue Mountains, fields to be plowed, an irrigation ditch to be dug, and adobes to be made. Besides all this, the Whitmans were busy learning the Nez Percé language and teaching the Indians the rudiments of agriculture, writing, and Christianity.[92] Finally, and always, Whitman was forever ready to ride to wherever serious illness or injury awaited him, whether to Walla Walla to treat Pierre Pambrun's Indian wife, or to deliver Eliza Spalding of a baby at Lapwai.

Whitman had chosen poorly for his house site. The spring floods of the Walla Walla repeatedly attacked the adobe foun-

dations, especially the cellar walls that he had attempted to dig under the house. When he realized his error, he began work on a second, much larger structure, a T-shaped building that has come down in history as the mission house.

But work on this new building went slowly at first; there was simply too much else to get done. Finally, a singular individual, Asahel Munger, arrived at the mission one day from the United States. Munger, his wife, suffering from poor health, and another couple had ridden west convinced they were so directed by the Lord to save the heathens. By the time they reached Waiilatpu, they realized they could not continue to survive in the hard land as independent missionaries. Munger willingly agreed to revert to his former calling of carpenter and to work on the mission house. However, for poor Munger it was already too late. Even while building window sills and laying floors he became deranged. The record describes the pathetically hilarious scene of Munger trying to give close-order drill to a group of insolent Indians. A few months later, in the Willamette Valley, he ended his earthly suffering by immolating himself in a fire, certain to the end that an ever-powerful God would rescue him.

Munger's skills were urgently needed when, in the fall of 1838, seven additional missionaries and William Gray's new wife arrived at Waiilatpu rather unexpectedly. Narcissa was of a mixed mind; it was wonderful having people fresh from home to learn all the happenings of the past two years, but it was a serious problem finding room for so many newcomers that late in the season.

The winter of 1838-39 was a most difficult one at Waiilatpu. Besides the three Whitmans in the small first house, were tall, stuttering Elkanah and vocal, cheerful Mary Walker; solemn, pious Cushing and frail, nervous Myra Eells; quarrelsome but intelligent Asa and sickly, homesick Sarah Smith; and the pleasant, even-tempered bachelor, Cornelius Rogers. By December, one or two rooms of the new mission house were sufficiently finished for the Smiths to move into it. But this eased the pressure very little, for Mary Walker now gave birth to her first-born.

The familiarity was too much. The winter weeks were

Elkanah and Mary Walker, two of the new missionary arrivals, as they looked in the late 1840s. (Elkanah from John Mix Stanley 1847 painting, Mary from daguerreotype. OHS Collections.)

marked with growing irritations and disputes, great and small. There began that winter irritating feuds that later would almost cause a premature ending to Waiilatpu and Lapwai. Marcus and Narcissa escaped the tensions of their own home for a few weeks by taking a winter camping trip to the Snake River. At the mouth of the Tucannon River, Marcus taught a band of Nez Percés wintering there and learned more of their language. Narcissa gave her attention to two-year-old Alice Clarissa.

With the coming of spring, the reinforcements moved out to the new stations at Tshimakain among the Spokan Indians and at Kamiah in the Nez Percé country, upriver on the Clearwater from Lapwai. Nevertheless, the seeds of discord already had been planted.

Although Whitman was not an ordained minister and therefore did not have as much ecclesiastical authority as the others, his strength of character and tremendous energies made him the natural leader of the missionaries, although not all the others accepted this fact gracefully. Also, Waiilatpu's strategic location — close to Fort Walla Walla and the British route of travel on the Columbia, and on the soon-to-be-crowded Oregon Trail and its Americans — made it the headquarters of the four mission stations. This proved to be both its blessing and its curse. It was good in that it provided the American Board with a focal point, an address in the wilderness as it were. For those undertakings that could be consolidated, it was usually Waiilatpu that became the site of operations.[93] But its location was a hindrance to the primary purpose of Waiilatpu — to bring Christianity to the Indians. This bothered both Marcus Whitman and the American Board in Boston. The latter never fully realized that Whitman could not help but devote a considerable amount of his time and efforts to the emigrants. Whitman never ceased trying to explain that he had no choice.

Along with the developments and improvements at the end of the 1830's, tragedy came to Waiilatpu. Alice Clarissa had been the first child born of United States citizens in the Pacific Northwest. Like her mother's successful journey and her father's coaxing a wagon as far west as Fort Boise, her birth had been a landmark in the history of emigration, for it proved that a family could be reared in the unknown country. Then, in June

1839, just 27 months old, Alice Clarissa Whitman drowned in the Walla Walla River, only a few feet from the door of her home. Partly because she had no more children of her own and partly because of her rarely relieved loneliness, Narcissa was many years recovering from the utter despair Alice's death brought her.

This black period manifested itself in many ways, including a growing dislike of the "filthy" Indians and a doubting of her own fitness for Oregon. It was magnified by poor physical health, by Marcus' absence for nearly a year, and by the trauma caused from an attempted assault on her person.[94] Not until the arrival of the seven Sagers in 1844 and their demands on Narcissa's time and energies, did she cease to be despondent and begin to live again. With eleven children to care for by then, she gave up even the pretense of being a missionary and, with a clear conscience, renewed her contract with life as a wife and mother.

Alice's death was a heavy blow to Marcus too. But his nature forbade an explosion of grief. He reported his daughter's death to the American Board, making it seem almost as an afterthought so as to hide his grief. Only rarely did he again refer to his dead daughter in writing.

There were more than enough problems at hand these years to occupy fully the doctor's attention. Nearly all the missionaries were fighting with one another. Nearly all of them, too, were writing letters to the American Board describing in detail the shortcomings of their fellow workers. The alarmed Secretaries became convinced that a change was necessary in Oregon. Out of the confusion of charges and countercharges, the following seemed clear to the Board: Asa Smith and William Gray were wholly dissatisfied with their lot, Gray because he sought vainly for a brighter place in the sun, Smith because he had lost confidence in the ability of the missions to succeed. Cushing Eells and Elkanah Walker got along with each other the best of any pair in the group. Their station at Tshimakain seemed a virtual haven of harmony in an angry sea. Henry Spalding, even at his erratic best, seemed to be showing the first symptoms of a disoriented mind. He was not dangerous, but he made things difficult for the others with his intense feelings and

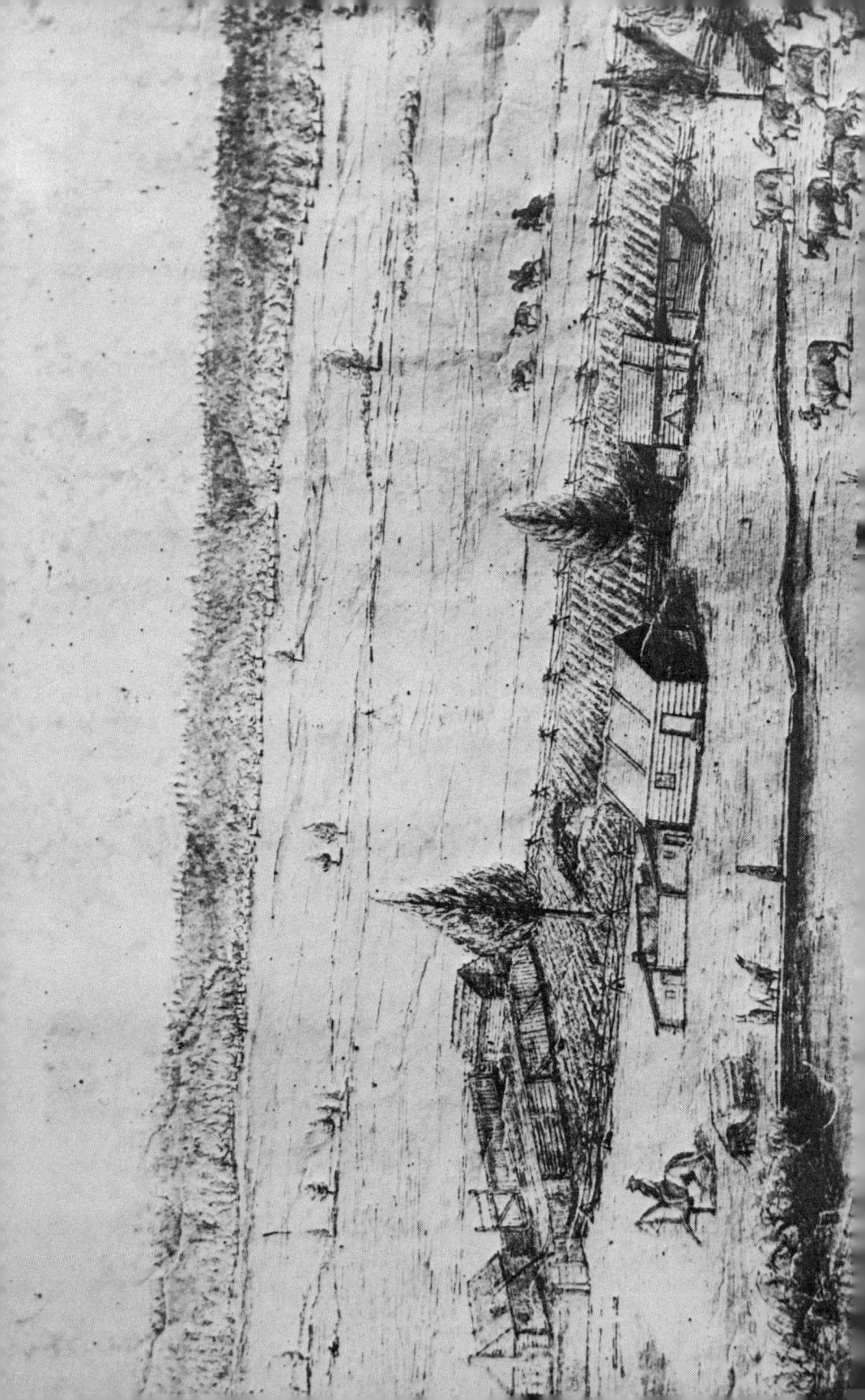

occasionally wild decisions. Then there was Marcus. His stubbornness and impatience saved him from being a paragon of virtue. But of them all, he seemed to be the pillar of stability, the moderator, and the natural leader.[95] If only they could get him away from Waiilatpu, which now seemed to them to be little more than a public inn on a fast-growing highway.

The emigrant train of 1842 brought the Board's decisions to Waiilatpu. Whitman's and Spalding's stations were to be closed down. Whitman was directed to move to Tshimakain to work with Eells and Walker. Spalding, Gray, and Smith were ordered to return to the United States. In consternation, the missionaries met at Waiilatpu to consider the alarming directions. They decided not to carry out the instructions until they could notify the Board of the considerable improvements in spirit and endeavor that had already come about among the stations. Gray and Smith had already left the mission field. Spalding had come a long way in seeing his errors — temporarily at least. All had confessed their sins publicly and had forgiven one another. The Board should be told that more harmony prevailed in the field now than ever before. Lapwai and Waiilatpu must remain open. Spalding must be allowed to stay.

Patience was not one of Marcus Whitman's virtues. He could not bear to think of a year or more of indecision — the year it would take for their letter to get to the Board and for a reply to come back. He announced suddenly to his startled associates that he would ride east at once and personally bring the current situation to the attention of the Board. Reluctantly the other missionaries agreed with this seeming madness — a ride across the continent in the height of winter.

Whitman's successful winter journey was a remarkable feat of endurance in the annals of the American West. When he arrived in Boston, he persuasively argued his case before an unfriendly Board. The result was that Henry Spalding, Lapwai, and Waiilatpu would continue their respective roles in the Pacific Northwest.[96]

Whitman's return to Waiilatpu coincided with the Great Migration of 1843. This was the largest group of emigrants yet to make the long journey, the first to number nearly 1,000. Their

[57]

Tshimakain mission, 1843-44, as drawn by Charles A. Geyer. Drury indicates that the Eells lived in the central house, the Walkers at left. (Original at Washington State College.)

companies were also the first to take their wagons all the way from the Missouri to the Willamette. In their collective wisdom, they took advantage of Whitman's presence and employed him as both doctor and guide. In the latter, more difficult part of the journey, it was his encouragement that kept many of the emigrants moving and taking their wagons just one mile farther. By September he was home at Waiilatpu. All the precedents had been set now for the adventures of the Sagers and the other thousands who were to come that way.

A New Life

Captain Shaw had not been gone from Waiilatpu more than a few days when Marcus and Narcissa resolved all doubts about accepting the seven children. They realized that they did not want to send the boys to Tshimakain and that they would not want to give up the children in the spring. Whitman sent word of these decisions to Shaw and, later, wrote the American Board: "These last [the Sagers] we took into our own family & have them yet and shall [be] likely to keep them."[97]

At last, the Sagers' future seemed secure. The next three years at Whitman's mission were happy ones for the girls and, after some time had passed, the boys, older and more self-reliant, came to think of Waiilatpu as home. One student of this period has noted that the children possessed a "curious time-illusion" in that the Sager girls later talked of this brief period as if they had lived always with the Whitmans.[98] While this overstates their attitudes, especially Catherine's, who retained vivid memories of the trip west, it is indicative of how rapidly they were absorbed into the Whitman family.

Life at the mission was not all childhood games and fun. In the manner of the times and in accord with their beliefs, the Whitmans were stern parents and on occasion erred on the side of regimentation. The restrictions placed on the children at their play and in their chores would cause dissent in many American homes today. Henry and Naomi Sager had been good parents to their children, but the overland journey had robbed the youngsters of much of their discipline. "We had been so long without restraint," Catherine wrote, "that we had become very unruly and hard to manage."[99] This the doctor and his wife set out to correct by whatever means necessary, having had some experience in handling an unruly child when Helen Mar Meek had arrived in 1840. The girls later remembered the Whitmans' strict discipline well, especially Narcissa's, and it was "very different to the ways of the plains," wrote Matilda.

For the moment, however, the passing emigrants threw the mission into constant turmoil as the sick, the tired, and the curious came past to seek aid and supplies or just to visit. During those first few days the children had to look after themselves except that "The first thing Mrs. Whitman did was cut our hair, wash and scrub us."[100]

About a week later the Sagers were reunited when the Eads wagon arrived with the baby. For the next few days Narcissa ignored the confusion about her and turned nearly all her attention to the baby's care. "So we took her, a poor, distressed little object, not larger than three weeks old." She continued, "The first thing I did for her was to give her some milk and put her in the cradle. She drank a gill, she was so hungry, but soon cleared herself of it by vomiting and purging." Then she bathed the baby, dressed it in clean clothes, and started it on its way to health. With this lavish care the child thrived. Within a few months Narcissa looked back at that beginning with a little pride: "Now I suppose you think such a child would be troublesome nights, but it is not so with her." In the same letter she reported: "She has nothing to do but to grow, and that as fast as possible; she is as large or larger than her next older sister Louise was when she came here, then nearly three years old."[101]

The baby had been given the name Rosanna, after her maternal grandmother, by Naomi Sager out on the prairies. But now the older children told the Whitmans that they wanted her to have a new name that would honor their dead parents. Narcissa and Marcus agreed, and the baby was renamed Henrietta Naomi.

Even with the baby present, the first weeks were lonely ones for Catherine. She was still not well enough to run about and to explore the mission buildings with her brothers and sisters. Her injured leg still confined her to a corner of the kitchen where she looked after the baby from time to time and tried to keep out of everyone's way. She remembered this lonely period: "I thought I could never be happy there where everything was so strange, and shed many tears in solitude."[102]

But it was this semi-isolation that was to bind Catherine close to Mrs. Whitman. Once the fall migration had passed, Narcissa was able to give more time to the children, especially to Catherine. Because she was the oldest girl and was confined to the house so much, Catherine became Narcissa's confidant in household matters. "During the doctor's frequent absences, I sat reading to or conversing with her, and at night was her bedfellow," Catherine wrote in her own maturity when she was seeking to identify the roots of her past. "She often remarked that she could not get along without me."[103]

Elizabeth, the second of the five girls, had a different relationship with the Whitmans, both of whom she too came to regard highly. Having all the life of a seven-year-old and fewer responsibilities than her sister, she was filled with a mixture of curiosity, knowledge, innocence, and childish naughtiness. She quickly learned that as far as the girls were concerned, Dr. Whitman left all matters of discipline to his wife. She discovered she could tease the doctor yet escape punishment, and later recalled that he was "a very jolly, kindly man. He loved to romp with we children." When the girls got into mischief, Elizabeth wrote that Whitman's response was to turn his back and laugh, leaving Narcissa the job of correcting and scolding.[104]

Although Narcissa had her "jolly" times too, her sense of responsibility was never far away. With eleven charges, she quickly learned not to waste her energies in scolding excessively. Instead she used the trick of pointing her finger, either at the task to be done or at the accused malingerer. The children learned to respect that finger more than any command. Elizabeth, at whom it must have been pointed often since she described it so vividly, said: "The way we jumped when it was leveled at us, you would have thought her forefinger was a gun and was likely to go off."[105]

The other two girls, four-year-old Matilda Jane, and three-year-old Hannah Louise, accepted their new lot in life with all the good graces of ignorance. Their memories were still short-lived enough that the adjustment to a new home was easily accomplished. Although in later life Matilda recounted much of her three years at the mission, many of her earliest memories were really not hers but were learned from Catherine and Elizabeth.

John and Francis, along with Perrin Whitman, came under the jurisdiction of the doctor. Perrin and John were the same age, 14, and both assisted in the heavy work in the fields, with the animals, and at the grist mill. Unfortunately not a single word from John Sager's pen survived the massacre. This is most regrettable because his sisters remembered him as being an avid diary keeper. They implied that he was a quiet boy, always conscious of his responsibilities to the rest. While he could not compete with Perrin in speaking the Indians' language, he was of increasing value to Whitman as time passed. On the frontier one had almost reached manhood at fourteen.

Francis was the leading rebel among the Sagers. The deaths of his parents had hurt him. The succeeding months on the trail had created in him a sense of rebellion that did not lie easily under Narcissa's pointing finger, or Marcus' reasoning. The strict, orderly routine at Waiilatpu tested him severely throughout the winter, but his rebellion remained below the surface until the next spring.

As usual, winter did not come to the mission that year until December. Snow covered the Blue Mountains weeks before it came down into the Walla Walla Valley. But fog, rains, and cold nights forecast the snows long in advance of their coming. When the winter storms did arrive, suddenly and always unexpectedly, the snow evaporated from the valley leaving but a trace of moisture. The arrival of winter marked the start of another school term at Waiilatpu. This year the teacher was an immigrant from the Sagers' train, Alanson Hinman. Conscientious, properly religious, but of less than average competence, Hinman hired himself to the Whitmans to teach the mission children for the term, after which he too planned to go to the lower Columbia in the spring to seek his fortune. Catherine described him as "one of those small-souled tyrants that could take delight in torturing helpless children, and who, under a cloak of religion, hid a black licentious heart." Nonetheless, Hinman enjoyed the confidence of Mrs. Whitman who "thought that whatever a teacher did was right."[106]

During the weeks the school was in session, the children were relieved from most of their other chores. Whitman hired the help he could afford from the wagon train to perform the tasks of the mission so as to allow the children full time on their studies. Despite the isolation of Waiilatpu, the mission school was taken most seriously. Whitman had sent for the necessary supplies and texts from the United States, including slates, a blackboard, and a map of the world. The youngsters discovered they had to attend classes regularly from Monday morning to Saturday noon. It was Whitman's ambition to see this school become a permanent institution. It would eventually outlive the purpose of the mission, he thought, and be available for the settlers whenever they put down roots in the Columbia basin.

Besides the regular schoolwork, the mission children underwent intensive religious training. For Francis especially this was the grim side of mission life: morning and evening prayers, verses of scripture to memorize daily and to repeat on Sunday at a mass recitation, Bible classes every Saturday night, Sunday school and church services on Sunday, recitation of the Ten Commandments on Sunday nights, prayer meeting once a week, a mission meeting on the first Monday of each month, and so on. Sundays were the worst of all. On that day no work was done and, for a boy, no fun to be had. "Each sat down with his books and thus spent the time till breakfast. Those who could not read were supplied with pictures." But if Francis found this regime unbearable, Catherine came to enjoy the experience. In the three years at the mission she developed deeply religious convictions, so much so that she sometimes alarmed the adults by her seriousness.[107]

The narrowness of the approach to religious matters had many diverse results, not all of them dismal. Matilda Jane recalled the day Elizabeth asked a stranger about his denomination. "She came in and told us, 'There's a Methodist out there.' As we had never seen a Methodist, we looked at him in wonder; but soon found he was not dangerous, went and talked to him."[108]

Despite the Methodists and other dangers, spring came to the Walla Walla Valley in 1845 in the wondrous burst of green that is its eternal beauty. The new leaves on the cottonwood trees traced the paths of the streams across the valley floor, while wild flowers sprinkled their colors through the prairie grass. To the east, the still snowy crest of the mountains marked the boundary between the blue sky and the black forest. The mountains encircled the rich land with the promise of guardianship during the hot summer ahead. The sky's colors gave way

The Whitman mission in 1845, from William H. Jackson's watercolor. Though based solely on survivor's accounts and painted before archeological excavations, it is a fairly accurate depiction of the mission. (Courtesy Whitman Mission National Historic Site.)

each evening to the gold, red, and black sunsets that spread over the etched basaltic cliffs of the Wallula Gap to the west. Spring came up the Columbia Gorge, bringing with it the winds of rain and the promises of renewed life. The mission school was dismissed and quickly became another memory. And, further back, the hurt and loneliness of the past summer were already fading fast away. Except for Francis, the new season captured the enthusiasm of the mission children. It seemed wonderful to be young and to be alive at Waiilatpu.

With spring, the winter's holdover of immigrants packed worn belongings and moved on to the Willamette. With this departure, the mission children, from the youngest to the oldest, were given their summer tasks. Whitman's cultivated acreage was never large, but each year he grew as many crops as possible, both for the mission table and for the coming fall's wagon trains. The small income he got for the grains and vegetables he used to buy other essentials from Forts Walla Walla and Vancouver. The boys helped with the heavier tasks, such as plowing, planting, and hoeing. The girls had their duties too: washing, ironing, mopping floors, berry picking, and tending the vegetable garden.

Some of the duties were distasteful. Matilda particularly recalled bean picking as a burdensome task: "One of the jobs that I disliked in the fall was when he [Whitman] pulled up the white beans and every child was given a tin cup and told to pick up these beans with their hands. Every bean had to be saved." Perhaps not so distasteful but certainly challenging was the job of walking along the rows of corn, ringing little bells to scare away the crows.[109]

But the pleasures of summer were many also. As a part of their education, Narcissa took the children on nature walks near the mission. On these excursions the children were expected to learn the rudiments of botany and, intentionally or not, all of them were to acquire a love of nature and of the land. Catherine, Elizabeth, and Matilda wrote of this early-day conservation with a sense of delight. In addition, Mrs. Whitman planted flowers around the mission house and the girls spent many hours in them, not just weeding. "Mrs. Whitman taught us a love of flowers. We each had a flower garden, which we had

to weed and care for. She had my brothers take a tin case and gather flowers as they would ride over the country and on their return would press them. She taught us a great deal about things of that kind and instilled in us a love of the beautiful. They kept our minds busy and cultivated a feeling of reverence for Nature."[110]

Another summer delight was bathing. Although Alice Clarissa had drowned in the Walla Walla River, Narcissa was too strong a person to retain any lasting fears of the water. She wrote: "Every one of my girls go to the river all summer long for bathing every day before dinner, and they love it so well that they would as soon do without their dinner as without that."[111] On one occasion, a fright occurred that must have brought a flood of memories to Narcissa. Emma Hobson was bathing with the rest when she was swept away by the current. She saved herself by grabbing an overhanging branch, and an Indian pulled her out of the river. The children thereafter called that part of the river "Emma's Place."[112]

Besides bodily cleanliness there was the mission laundry. This was one of the big jobs of the week and from it few were excused. Rising at four in the morning of wash day, adults and children, boys and girls, assembled in the kitchen. The boys did most of the heavy work, such as bringing the water and pounding the clothes. But there was plenty of rubbing for the women, as well as hanging the clothes on the line, serving coffee, and getting the breakfast ready.[113] But during that first summer at the mission, the boys had to get along without the help of Francis Sager on washdays. He had run away.

Memorial Shaft Hill, adjacent to Whitman mission. Narcissa Whitman often took the Sager children on walks on this hill, where she taught them lessons in nature. The Sager girls continued to have a love for flowers, grasses, and trees in later life. (Courtesy Whitman Mission NHS.)

"As If They Were My Own"

The first winter at Waiilatpu was an unbearable period for twelve-year-old Francis. The sudden adjustment to the strict regimentation of the Whitman household after the freedom experienced during the months of travel was more than his young mind could accept patiently. To add to Francis' troubles, Hinman apparently decided to crush the boy's spirit and to make him malleable to his moods. In the name of education, the schoolmaster laid the whip to Francis for all and any misdemeanors. Even Catherine, who was loathe to criticize anyone associated with the mission, wrote: "He certainly bestowed upon my brother some of the most cruel whippings that it was ever the lot of boys to receive."[114]

A sympathetic but unidentified witness to Francis' predicament, known to posterity only as Mr. P., was the person whom Narcissa Whitman blamed for persuading Francis to leave the mission. Whoever he was, Mr. P. had talked to both John and Francis that winter, urging them to go down to the Willamette with the wintering wagons as soon as spring came.[115] John had turned down the idea, but Francis, almost ill from his punishments, decided to run away. Marcus Whitman was away on the day Francis left. As the boy prepared his departure, someone told Narcissa. Breakfast on that lonely day was eaten in silence. "Francis arose from the table, and, taking his hat, started for the door. Mrs. Whitman, starting from her seat, said in a mild, firm voice: 'Francis, you must not go; you must stay with me.' He replied, 'I must go. I can't stay.'" He left the kitchen, mounted his horse, and rode off before the winter stayovers' wagons were ready to roll.[116]

His sisters were saddened to see him leave, but Narcissa was chagrined. She talked with John and from him learned of the undermining of her efforts to manage the large family. Perhaps too she realized for the first time that Hinman's methods were anything but Christian. She was somewhat relieved to learn that John had resisted Mr. P.'s arguments and would remain with his sisters, although he too showed some resistance to the manner in which he and Francis had been treated. Narcissa knew that the story would rapidly spread throughout the American colony on the Willamette, and that John's staying would help soften the criticism that would be directed toward her and Marcus. Already the Whitmans had been the victims of immigrants' gossip, and it had not been a pleasant experience. Some had called Narcissa a "stuck-up redhead"; others had complained of the high price of Whitman's supplies, little realizing while still at Waiilatpu that prices would be higher yet in the Willamette Valley. New criticism would do the mission little good, although Narcissa was sincere when she said that criticism bothered her very little as a person. She had already received plenty of that, deserved or not, from her associates. However, the Whitmans failed to see that the real reason for Francis' departure was not themselves, but their insistence on defending the cruelty of Hinman, all in the name of Christianity.

As usual, Mrs. Whitman's instincts in this matter were correct. Before much time passed, a letter arrived from Mrs. William H. Brewer, the wife of one of the Methodist missionaries at The Dalles, the nearest American settlement downriver from Waiilatpu. Mrs. Brewer was full of news and questions. She told of the arrival of Francis. She had heard that Francis had run away because of the strict discipline. There was a suggestion too that Francis had resented deeply the Whitmans' attempt to baptize him earlier that spring. From someone she had learned also of the beatings that had occurred.

Narcissa's reply was defensive but moderate. She wrote: "I endeavor in all things to act towards the children as if they were my own. My sincere, ardent and abiding wish is to train them up for God and eternity." She noted their lack of discipline when they had first arrived but, thanks to Hinman's teaching, they all now had good habits of study. Far from censuring Hinman, she thought that "Some, or all of the older ones, are showing considerable mind and rather seriously inclined." As for the criticisms, "I do not think them difficult children to manage, neither do I have occasion often to use the rod. The little one, as all other little children do, manifested a stubborn disposition at first, which required subduing; since she has appeared well—obeys promptly when spoken to. I have no reason to regret the course I have pursued with her. . . . Doubtless this is what has occasioned the remarks [of beatings], for it took place about the time Francis went away. Louise, the next older, I have not been able to subdue so completely."[117]

In the next few years, Whitman, while never acknowledging in writing that he, Mrs. Whitman, or Hinman, might have been at fault, nonetheless began doing some long-overdue thinking about the Sagers' future. It had been on his mind for some time to take the necessary legal steps that would insure their future security. Oregon still did not belong to the United States in 1845, but that had not stopped the settlers in the Willamette from setting up a "provisional government" and a legal system of sorts. Whitman decided to visit the lower country in order to use this system to legalize his guardianship of the orphans.

First he had a long and serious talk with John. When the doctor was fully assured in his mind that John was content to remain at the mission, Whitman then proposed to help the boys acquire cattle and horses which they would raise at Waiilatpu.[118] This would give them a start in acquiring property which they would need when on their own. This and an education was all he could afford for them. As soon as Marcus and John worked out the details of this understanding, a letter and a horse were sent to Francis, along with an invitation to return.

Little is known of Francis' adventures in the Willamette, but the invitation to come home eventually proved stronger than whatever pleasures and excitement he found there. Also, Hinman left the mission later that summer, enroute for the Willamette. That fall, Francis returned to the mission where he came to terms with Narcissa's pointing finger. The incident was not again a matter of discussion, presumably much to the disappointment of the Willamette gossips.

Marcus Whitman made his visit to the Willamette Valley and there he called upon Captain Shaw and Judge James W. Nesmith. Nesmith was already one of early Oregon's leading citizens. Born in New Brunswick, Canada, of American parents, he had drifted westward like so many others, first to Missouri, then to Iowa. In 1843 he had been an "orderly sergeant" in that year's Great Emigration to Oregon. After reading law in the Oregon Country, he had become a supreme judge shortly before Whitman's visit. Later in life he was to represent Oregon in both the U. S. Senate and the House of Representatives and to acquire the rank of colonel in the Oregon militia. President U. S. Grant would have ideas of appointing him a justice of the U. S. Supreme Court, but Nesmith's politics would get in the way of that appointment.

For now, the three men discussed the Sager situation and a court order was drawn up formally appointing Dr. Whitman as guardian of the children. That such a document could be prepared in 1845 showed how far the development of the Oregon Country had come in the ten years since American settlement of any extent had begun:

Klackamas District
3d June, 1845   J. W. Nesmith, Judge

Now on this day came Marcus Whitman, of this district, and represents as follows: That Henry Sager, late of the State of Missouri, died, as it is said, on or about the 30th day of August, 1844, while on his journey immigrating to Oregon, and that one William Shaw did then take possession and charge of the goods, chattels and effects of the said Henry Sager, which were as follows: John C. Sager, Francisco Sager, Catherine Sager, Elizabeth M. Sager, and Matilda Jane Sager and Hannah L. Sager, and Henrietta Sager, all, it is said, under the age of fourteen years, and furthermore, that the said William Shaw did, on the 6th day of November, 1844, deliver to Marcus Whitman at his station, all the goods, chattels and effects belonging to the estate of the aforementioned Henry Sager, deceased, together with the aforesaid children, all to remain with said Marcus Whitman until further arrangements could be made.

And now the said Marcus Whitman requests that a guardian may be appointed to said orphans by the court, and also that measures may be taken to secure the estate of Henry Sager, deceased, for the use and benefit of his heirs.

Whereupon the court appointed B. Nichols, Solomon Eads to the said Marcus Whitman. The appraisers, after being and Edmund B. Magruder to appraise and fix the value of said estate of the said Henry Sager at the date it was delivered up sworn, returned the bill of appraisement, which amounted to the sum of $262.50.

Whereupon the said Marcus Whitman gave bond for double the above sum and was appointed guardian of the above named children, subject to, and accountable to, the probate judge of Oregon.

(Signed) J. W. Nesmith
Probate Judge of Oregon.[119]

The three appraisers appointed by the court drew up a list of the Sagers' pathetic possessions. In terms of dollars, Henry Sager had left his children a very small inheritance:

APPRAISAL of estate of Henry Sager delivered to Marcus Whitman by Wm Shaw on the 6th of Nov. 1844

3 yoke of oxen at $50 per yoke	150.00
The fore wheels of one wagon	13.00
One cow	37.50
One odd steer	29.00
One cow (excluding five dollars expended in procuring her from the Indians)	20.00
3 chains and two yokes	10.00
1 ax	2.00
1 screw plate	3.00
	262.50 [*sic*]

June 25, 1845

Benjamin Nichols
Solomon Eads
Com. B. Magruder[120]

The year 1845 had begun quietly at Waiilatpu as far as the Cayuses were concerned. The Indians who lived in the vicinity visited the mission often, and the children quickly learned their names and began to pick up a smattering of their language, although Narcissa tried to discourage this. To her the ordinary earthy Indian speech was too often obscene. In February, the Whitmans wrote the Walkers at Tshimakain saying that everything seemed to be going well in their relations with the Cayuses. It was true that very few converts had been made and that Mrs. Whitman had withdrawn from missionary work to look after her family. Nonetheless the Indians seemed content to have Whitman live among them, still struggling to convert them to his religion and to his way of life. Some of them were making a small income by selling crops and trading cattle and horses with the immigrants each fall. As long as these whites did not stop to settle on Cayuse lands, the Indians did not seem to worry. But even as Whitman wrote Walker, a band of Cayuses, Walla Wallas, and Spokans had traveled all the way to California to trade some of its fine horses for more cattle.

Just seven years earlier, John A. Sutter had ridden west in company with the reinforcements for the American Board stations. Much had happened to him since then and he was now one of the leading Americans in Mexico's California. The Indians from the Columbia had arrived at Sutter's great fort on the Sacramento River. There, the son of the principal leader of the Walla Wallas was killed by a white man in a dispute over a mule. By the end of February these Indians had returned home, without their cattle, and greatly angered by the death. The quietness of Waiilatpu changed overnight to an intense excitement. On March 5, Whitman wrote Walker again: "You will get the news of the California affair from Garry. We are to have a great assembly of Indians at W. W. next week."[121] Within a week, Walker wrote in his diary that the hotter heads among the Indians were talking of revenge by killing Whitman and Factor Archibald McKinley at Fort Walla Walla.[122]

This excitement was still pretty much the state of affairs when the missionaries gathered at Waiilatpu for their annual meeting in May.[123] This was the first opportunity the Sagers had to meet the Walkers, Eellses, and Henry Spalding. And it was these missionaries' first chance to size up the additions to the mission family. Despite Francis' absence, the missionaries were favorably impressed with the children.[124] In contrast to past meetings, this one proceeded smoothly. Even the crisis concerning the Indians failed to dampen the good spirits and hopes for the future expressed by all the members. Gone was most of the bickering of the earlier years and much of the past stalemated business was now completed, such as granting letters of dismissal to Smith and Gray who had left the mission three years earlier.

From Mary Walker's diary, we learn of the new business undertaken: "Sun. [May] 11. A church meeting in the morning. Mr. Hinman was examined for admission to the church." Still on Sunday, "Mr. Hinman was baptized. Dr. Whitman had the five orphan sisters & Mary Ann B. baptized." On the following day, Hinman put on a display of his temperament by having fits, "occasioned probably by excitement on the sabbath." This occurrence may well have reinforced John Sager's reluctance to join his sisters in being baptized.[125] Francis, by his absence, missed his opportunity to protest.

That autumn, with Francis home again, the mission prepared for the onslaught of immigrants who were again pouring across the Blue Mountains. This fall, by circumstances rather than by design, an immigrant came to Whitman's door who was to have a great influence on the mission children. He was Andrew Rodgers, who was to replace Hinman as the mission teacher.

Rodgers came to Oregon with a friend who was already seriously afflicted by tuberculosis. Like so many others, the sick man hoped to find a cure in the dry western climate. Like so many others, he was already deadly ill by the time the caravan reached the Umatilla, and was too ill to travel farther. Rodgers brought his companion to the mission in the vain hope that Marcus could heal him. As they had done so often before, the Whitmans took the sick man into their home and nursed him with great concern. But the disease was too far advanced and the patient died. In those few weeks Rodgers had shown himself to be a man of good character and of strong religious convictions. The Whitmans asked him to stay on at the mission. He agreed and took Hinman's former position at Waiilatpu as teacher.

Rodgers soon won the children's affection as well as their respect, and he fully gained the confidence and highest regard of both Marcus and Narcissa. He had been a member of a Secessionist church back in the States, but had been expelled for singing and for playing a violin. Now he could enjoy both these pleasures, and Narcissa had a friend whose musical talent and training were as great as hers. Together she and Rodgers sang many a duet to the delight of the mission. Rodgers taught the children singing too, and a choir was formed for Sunday and prayer services that was of no mean ability.

Marcus was taken with Andrew's convictions on religion. With Whitman's encouragement, Rodgers began preparing himself for the ministry while living at the station. Marcus even requested the Board to send a long list of books for Rodgers to study. Within a year, Narcissa was able to write: "Mr. Rodgers acts as our minister and maintains the station with considerable dignity."[126]

Catherine was the only one of the sisters to describe Rodgers. She remembered him as "a young man of about twenty-five, tall and slender, with a thin, sallow complexion, denoting bad health. His hair was sandy from which he derived his Indian name, Hushus Muk Muk (Yellow Head)." But Rodgers' health remained good and for the next two years he was an active member of the mission family. Despite continued threats against the mission from the discontented element among the Cayuses, Rodgers preferred life with the Whitmans to the unknown fortunes of the Willamette.

When Rodgers arrived at Waiilatpu, Whitman was swiftly moving to a showdown with the Indians. By November, the malcontents were accusing Whitman of being responsible for the various illnesses in the tribe and for the death of the Walla Walla chief's son at Sutter's Fort. Moreover, they were sure that Whitman was secretly plotting to take over the Cayuse lands.

Cyrus Walker, Elkanah's seven-year-old son who was born at Waiilatpu, returned that winter to attend Rodgers' school. He recalled many years later the tensions at the mission. "One day, during the winter, as Catherine and Elizabeth Sager, and perhaps Eliza Spalding, were ironing in the kitchen, an Indian, a brother of Tomahas, or 'the Murderer,' as he is called, came in, and picking up a flatiron proceed[ed] to iron his handkerchief, against which the girls protested.[127] I can remember his angry looks as he advanced toward Elizabeth Sager, I think it was, and threatened to kill her. Mrs. Whitman pacified him by telling him they were only girls, and not to pay any attention to them."[128] This is one of the few recorded instances in which Narcissa Whitman bowed down to the insolence of an Indian. If this story is basically correct, Elizabeth had something to occupy her thoughts during spells of daydreaming in school that winter.

Whitman finally met with those Cayuses who were making threats against his life. Because of the increased activity of the Catholic missions in the Columbia basin, he was reluctant to give up Waiilatpu. However, he realized that the mission work could not continue under a constant volley of threats. He told the Cayuses that he would give them until spring to decide whether or not they wished Waiilatpu to continue as an American Board mission. If they so desired then, he would leave their country forever. In his heart he hoped they would want him to stay.[129]

As far as the children were concerned, the winter of 1845-46 passed in much the same manner as had the previous one. Mr. Rodgers kept them busier at their studies than even Hinman had, but with fewer beatings. About the only excitement that interrupted the routine, besides Elizabeth's problem with the iron, was the scandal that Cyrus Walker got himself into. It seems he had a seven-year-old's healthy curiosity about sex, especially the opposite. Although the record is careful not to disclose exactly what happened, it appears that Cyrus expressed this curiosity to some of the girls. Then someone told.

When his mother found out the following spring, she was mortified. Indeed her good friend, Myra Eells, forbade her own boys from playing with Cyrus for fear he would contaminate them with his evil ways.[130] But good sense prevailed in the end, at least at Waiilatpu, and Narcissa and Marcus invited Cyrus back for the following winter's term. However the Walkers thought it prudent to teach Cyrus at home. None could have known it, but one outcome of this decision was that Cyrus was not at Waiilatpu when disaster struck in November 1847, thus escaping a virtually certain death.

The year 1846 was in every respect, except for the conversion of the Indians, the best year the mission had seen since its earliest days. The Indians did not again demand Marcus' removal when spring came. Narcissa's health and spirits had not been so excellent since before Alice Clarissa's death. Indeed, all seemed to be at peace and Waiilatpu was serene. Mary Walker was disappointed to learn that Dr. Whitman's horse had fallen on him, hurting his knee, and he would not be present for the birth of her latest child. He sent his best advice however: "Let Nature take its unobstructed course which is all the physician aims as far as possible."[131] Mary did fine, as usual, without the doctor's presence.

Narcissa's state of mind that summer was one of busy bliss. In a letter home she described her happy circumstances: "I have six girls sewing around me, or rather five — for one is reading, and the same time my baby [Henrietta] is asking me to go and bathe—she is two years the last of May. . . . Now comes another with her work for me to fix. So it is from morning to evening. . . . I could get along easier if I could bring my mind to have them spend their time in play, but this I cannot." She continued: "Now all the girls have gone to bathe and this will give me time for a few moments to close my letter in peace; they are very good girls and soon will be more help to me than they are now, although at present they do considerable work."[132]

If Narcissa's love for her family was evident, it was never far removed from her sense of responsibility. "I avoid as much as possible giving my children candies, sweetmeats, etc., such as many parents allow . . . neither do I permit them to eat cakes and pies very often." She wrote too: "If children complain of the headache, or are sick at the stomach, send them to bed without their supper; they are sure to get up very soon feeling as well as ever. My husband says," she added authoritatively, "many times when a physician is called to see a patient he finds nothing ails him but eating too much."[133]

With the school year over, the children resumed their summer tasks. Despite Narcissa's worry about letting them play too much, they managed to have a sufficient number of adventures before the summer was over. On one occasion they took oxen and a wagon and went on a camping trip in the direction of the Blue Mountains, toward the sawmill in the foothills. This was about a 15-mile journey up Mill Creek. Selecting a site of scenic beauty, the adventurers set up their camp and turned out the oxen to graze. In the morning they discovered the oxen had gone home during the night. Undoubtedly the expedition could have spent the day hiking home, but the woods and streams were too pleasant. Surely if they stayed long enough, someone would come looking for them. They reinforced the now meager food supply by catching a salmon, which they made into soup. That night they said their prayers under the starry sky and again slept amid the haunting cry of the coyote. It was like being on the Oregon Trail again, only this time there was more fun and no hurry to go anywhere. On the third morning, one of the Sager boys, probably John, came looking for them and returned them safely to the mission, none the worse for their wilderness experience.[134]

On another fine summer day, Matilda, who seemed to have a knack for being where trouble was, and an unnamed sister took the cows out to pasture. The two girls amused themselves by looking along the path for the different herbs they had seen

[77]

Indians eat. They spotted one plant about which a mild argument ensued. One of the girls said that the Indians ate it, the other said the plant was poisonous. Matilda settled the argument by eating some. She promptly took ill, managed to stagger home, and collapsed in the doorway. Everyone was certain she was dying, but with Mrs. Whitman's care, she recovered completely.[135]

During this time of worry over Matilda, John Sager, concerned about his sister's recovery, found himself falling under Narcissa's spell. Prior to this he had kept aloof, resisting her more open overtures to friendship, yet resisting the rebellious spirit that had conquered Francis. Now "he began to look upon her differently," observed Catherine, "and to receive her rebukes as meant for his good."[136]

So passed the hot days of the summer of 1846. As Narcissa said, "I must be with them or else they will be doing something they should not."[137] When autumn came the Walkers and the Eellses prepared Tshimakain for company.[138] It was their turn to host the annual mission meeting. But on the agreed date no visitors came from either Waiilatpu or Lapwai. Mary Walker was somewhat alarmed, but an explanation soon arrived by messenger. There would be no annual meeting. Marcus Whitman could not leave Waiilatpu because the immigrant trains were arriving, and there was too much sickness among the travelers for him to get away. Thus began the terrible winter of 1846-47, the worst in the still short history of the Oregon Country.

Before the fury of the winter passed, thousands of Indian horses and many of their cattle lay dead and frozen. Fear, despair, and unrest spread through the tribes. It did not help the missionaries' cause that they had been more provident and had suffered less. White men were always suffering less. The Cayuses, especially, felt sorry for themselves at the expense of the Whitmans' foresightedness. The winter's disasters were climaxed when word came in April about the Donner tragedy in the Sierra Nevada of California.[139] These were dead white men, but their deaths did nothing to ease the suffering and losses of the Indians on the Columbia plateau. It was a winter that men everywhere in the West would remember. And among the Cayuses it would be remembered as the winter for whose disasters Marcus Whitman was somehow responsible.

The postponed meeting was held at Tshimakain in June, 1847. Narcissa, whose health had improved immeasurably, decided to make the long trip.[140] She had not been so far from home since 1843. As an unusual treat, Catherine was to go also. This was her longest trip since she had arrived in Oregon. With much excitement, she, Mrs. Whitman, and Andrew Rodgers traveled northward with Cushing Eells, who had come down to Waiilatpu.

Across the Palouse hills and the smoke-green Snake River the party rode north, traveling a little out of its way to visit the powerful Palouse Falls in their forbidding but fascinating setting. As soon as they arrived at Tshimakain, just north of the pine-bordered Spokane River, all were invited to the Eells' house for supper. For the next ten days Catherine played with the Eells and Walker children, helped care for the smaller ones, and even attended some of the women's meetings with Narcissa. It was at this time that Mary Walker observed the intensity of Catherine's public praying.[141] Meanwhile, the men reached the important decision that they would purchase Wascopam at the Dalles of the Columbia, the last active Methodist Indian mission in Oregon. Pressure was put on Elkanah Walker to leave Tshimakain to manage the Dalles station. He resisted but finally agreed to travel down the Columbia to look it over. Later, after seeing it, he refused to move; as a result relations between him and Whitman were quite strained that summer and fall.[142]

Catherine's description of the all-but-forgotten Tshimakain mission has survived: "The houses were built of logs," in contrast to Waiilatpu's adobe buildings, "and situated but a short distance apart. The yards were piled in with slabs to protect the poultry from the ravages of the Indian dogs. Out of the side of a hill in front of Mr. Eells' house a spring gushed out and was carried in troughs to the house. The land around the station was flat and skirted with pine timber, and a beautiful stream of water ran through it. It was a lovely place."[143]

Shortly after Catherine returned to Waiilatpu with the Whitmans, John was sent to the Dalles with a hired man and two wagons to bring back supplies that had been shipped by sea from the American Board. This was an adult's job and it demonstrated that the 17-year-old was now in manhood. John had a successful trip and returned with a new threshing machine, a cornsheller, plows for the Indians, and general goods for the mission.[144]

Late that summer, Whitman traveled down to the Willamette to arrange for the transfer of the Dalles mission to the American Board. While in the valley, he called upon William Shaw to report on the health and welfare of the seven Sagers. He told Shaw he was planning on formally adopting the girls and changing their name to Whitman. Shaw demurred. He reminded Whitman that Henry Sager had been his good friend and somehow it did not seem to be right that Henry's offspring should have another name. Whitman finally agreed. But he still wanted to adopt the girls so that they could inherit whatever estate he might have. He did not get around to taking out the adoption papers on that trip; but the girls were to believe ever after that they were the adopted children of the Whitmans.[145]

While returning to the mission, Whitman scouted along the south bank of the Columbia for a better wagon road for that fall's immigrants, whose vanguard was already trickling down the slopes of the Blue Mountains. By keeping inland from the river, and thus avoiding the growing number of thieving river Indians who found it profitable to prey on wagons, he found such a trail and marked it for the newcomers. Then he hastened home to prepare for the onslaught of whites, and to try to quiet the growing restlessness of the Cayuses. Whitman knew that this fall would be a landmark in his relations with the Indians and, one way or another, the watershed in the history of the Oregon mission.

Tension

Several times in the past two years, Marcus Whitman had given serious thought to giving in to Indian threats, closing the Waiilatpu mission, and moving to the Willamette Valley. He realized that the Cayuses were doomed to extinction. Even if the Indians survived the impact from the thousands of whites pouring across their lands annually, it was only a matter of a few years before these newcomers would occupy the Columbia basin and would destroy any obstacles to their prosperity. It was the old story that had already been heard across the eastern half of the nation. Doubtlessly, the tragedy would soon come to this newest land.

In the earlier years, it had seemed possible to Marcus that he could teach these people a way of life by which to survive the onslaught, teach them not just white man's Christianity but a way of living, a settled farming economy in which the Indians would adapt themselves to a permanent-type community. If they could grasp that idea and carry it to its maximum possibilities, then they might be able to resist the whites — resist them not by arms but by the very existence of their own thriving ranches, churches, and homes. That dream had vanished; pragmatism had largely replaced idealism in Whitman. Still he held on to the mission. In the end, he solved each crisis by deciding to hang on just a little longer. His commitment to the Cayuses caused him to reject the idea of quitting; he would try just once more to find success — for himself, and for the Indian.

There were other, lesser reasons besides his conscience that caused Whitman to hang on. There was the annual migration to consider. While most of the newcomers went on to the lower Columbia without his assistance, there were each fall those who would have died before reaching the Willamette had it not been for Waiilatpu. There were no other American communities, let alone medical doctors, to which these destitute and sick could turn. If Whitman were to leave Waiilatpu, the unfortunates of the trail would not reach their goal.

Then there were the Catholic missionaries. In 1847, there was no ecumenical spirit. There was no love between priest and preacher. The Roman Catholic and Protestant churches were bitter rivals for men's souls in all the mission fields, and Oregon was no exception. If Marcus gave up Waiilatpu, it would probably be occupied immediately by newly appointed Bishop A. M. A. Blanchet of (Fort) Walla Walla.[146] A number of the Indians were quick to take advantage of this rivalry. They became expert at playing upon the sensibilities of both groups of missionaries when they could foresee material gain for themselves.[147]

Two years earlier, the Indians had threatened Whitman's life; but that crisis had passed in due course. Whitman felt, even now, that if the Cayuses should carry out such a threat, only his life would be at stake. His correspondence shows that he never thought that Narcissa or the children would be endangered.

Students of the event of that fall in 1847 have been able to trace back a multitude of grievances and troubles, large and small, real and imaginary, that may have played a role in the momentous climax that was about to happen.[148] But out of all the grievances and misunderstanding two emerge predominately: the problem of trying to force an alien culture on the Indians, and the measles epidemic of 1847.

The basic problem was simple but insoluble—two cultures trying to occupy the same place. The Cayuses knew what had happened elsewhere when white immigrations had arrived. They counted the increasingly larger wagon trains each fall with alarm. They feared the day the settler would stop on Cayuse land. This would eventually happen, for Tom Hill had told them so.

Tom Hill was a dispossessed, English-speaking Delaware Indian who knew well the results of white occupation. Forced westward, he had become a part of the glorious era of the mountain men. In the Rocky Mountains he had acquired a Nez Percé wife. When the fur trade declined, he had come down into Nez Percé country to live with these horsemen of the plateau. He became acquainted with the missionaries and, while he had respect for them as persons, he foresaw in their presence disaster for the Nez Percés and their neighbors.

Hill could speak with great eloquence and gradually his concepts took hold among the non-Christian Nez Percés, who always admired an orator, until he was accepted by them as one of their most important leaders. Because of this power and because of his anti-white arguments, the missionaries came to fear Tom Hill and to consider him as a person determined to thwart their purpose. Yet in the light of history, Hill must be considered a prophet and, perhaps, a patriot. It is hardly surprising that all his dread prophecies eventually came true when, 30 years later, Chiefs Looking Glass, Joseph, and the rest tried to lead their people to salvation only to be crushed.

But Hill was not a red saint. On a much lower plane, he sowed trouble for Whitman and Spalding when he argued that they were getting rich at the expense of the Indians. He persuaded many of his followers that because of this they should either force the missionaries to leave, or at least charge them heavy rent.

The Nez Percés were not the only ones influenced by Hill. A strong element of the non-Christians in the Cayuse tribe paid heed to him also. When the son of Peupeumoxmox, the principal chief of the Walla Walla tribe, was killed in California in 1845 and eventually Whitman got the blame, it was Tom Hill that Whitman had to deal with as well as Tomahas and the infuriated leaders of the Cayuses and the Walla Wallas.

Catherine Sager, not fully aware of all the implications nor quite understanding the problems at that time, nonetheless left a detailed description of Whitman's meeting with Tom Hill. The doctor invited Hill and his followers to a feast at the mission and treated them in the fashion of the day in the "Indian room" or meeting room in the main mission house. "A fire was kindled in the yard, and a large kettle holding near 20 gallons was suspended over it," wrote Catherine, who was participating in her first and only great feast. "This was to prepare the mush, the indispensable article of an Indian table."

When Whitman had seated himself as master of ceremonies, "The chiefs sat around the kettle," which had been placed in the Indian room, "and the others filed in according to their rank or standing. While the Doctor and chiefs dipped their spoons into the kettle, the others were served with vessels which they held in their hands, meat, bread, etc., being handed to them by those who acted as waiters." The mission children were amused to see how greatly the Indians craved sugar, "wanting their tea made as sweet as sugar itself." Despite the serious aspects of the feast, the children began to giggle at some of the mannerisms of their guests. Narcissa would not tolerate disrespectful behavior and she "would have to send us out to indulge our mirth."

The meal over, "Tom Hill was the orator of the evening. He spoke for two or three hours. I heard the speech spoken of very highly by the Doctor, his wife, and Mr. Rodgers, but unfortunately I am in ignorance as to the subject of his discourse." On the other hand, Catherine retained a vivid image of Hill's commanding appearance: "Tom was richly and gorgeously dressed on this occasion, in full Indian costume. His hunting shirt was of deerskin, stained slightly red, cut full of holes and fringed. This was worn over a striped shirt. His pants were of the same material as his hunting shirt, fringed down the side. His feet were encased in moccasins decorated with porcupine quills; and his long hair hung around his shoulders."[149]

But in this fall of 1847, there was no Tom Hill for Whitman to negotiate with. He had gone to California with the second Cayuse-Walla Walla expedition. His purpose in going may have been to join his old mountain days friend, Kit Carson, who was assisting Frémont in the struggle for California.[150] The Cayuses did not need Tom Hill this year to give them prophecies or reasons for their deeds. They could see for themselves that Marcus Whitman was becoming increasingly involved with the immigrants. They did not realize, just as the American Board did not, that Whitman had no moral choice. The immigrants were there, they needed supplies and medical help, and Whitman had to supply these needs. The Cayuses knew only that Whitman had less time and energy to spend on their behalf. They sensed a change in the mission's efforts, and they lost faith in its purpose for being. Increasingly, they believed Whitman to be more an agent for the whites than a missionary and teacher for themselves. Jealousy and fear clouded their minds.

The immediate catalyst that brought disaster to Waiilatpu was made known to Whitman while he was surveying the new trail on his return from Vancouver that fall. The first horsemen and wagons to cross the Blues told the doctor that a great measles epidemic had spread through the wagon trains. They also informed him that there were almost 5,000 travelers that year, the largest number yet to make dust on the Oregon Trail.

As Whitman hastened back to Waiilatpu, he realized that the measles would bring great complications to an already delicate balance. This was a white man's disease and the Indians' bodies did not have the generations of resistance to it that the whites did. A white child might become seriously ill from the measles, but its chances of recovery were good. He feared that when the disease spread through the tribe, as it would do, the result would be death.

His greatest fears were realized. There are no accurate figures on how many Cayuses died that autumn from the measles and the accompanying dysentery. The highest figure that has been given, and the one most commonly accepted, is that about one-half of the tribe died in less than two months. Even if the actual figure was less than that, the disease was great enough to spread panic among the Cayuses. The cornered, frightened people were ready to slash out at the cause of their predicament. The Indians sought out Whitman as the man who, in their eyes, had brought this death.

Ever since his first year among the Cayuses, Whitman had known that as a doctor he walked a delicate path. For untold generations it had been the custom in the Cayuse tribe to reward a successful medicine man, or *tewat,* with honor and riches, and to kill the unsuccessful *tewat* in justified revenge. During the past eleven years the Whitmans and the other missionaries had recorded the incidents in which the relatives of the deceased had revenged his spirit by killing the *tewat.* This was not murder; it was a right.[151] However, for these eleven years, Whitman had prayerfully walked the tightrope between success and failure due his profession. He had managed to avoid being drawn into this labyrinth of superstition. Now, though he worked desperately day and night to ease the suffering among the Indians, the immigrants, and in his own family, he was losing the fight. Panic-stricken, the Cayuses lost completely their faith in his medicine. They turned to their traditional methods and treated their fevers by taking a sweat bath, then plunging into an icy stream. Although this usually assured their immediate death, it did not absolve Whitman from his failures. In the survivors' minds they had the right to kill *Tewat* Whitman.

While there was no Tom Hill to sway the Cayuses either way in their councils, there was Joe Lewis. Hill, argumentative but intelligent, controversial but compromising, would have rejected the arguments attributed to Lewis were he still on the Columbia. Lewis was an unprincipled scoundrel who saw personal gain in spreading discontent. He had told Whitman that he had been born in Canada, raised in Maine, and had fought with Frémont in California during the Mexican War. Joining an immigrant train at Fort Hall he had been a troublemaker on the way to Waiilatpu, where the immigrants had got rid of him by refusing to take him farther.[152] As with all strays, outcasts, and misfits of all the autumns, the Whitmans took in Lewis and provided him with his needs. Before many days had passed, the missionaries reluctantly concluded that to keep Lewis any longer was courting disaster. He could only increase the burdens and troubles that now beset the mission from every side. Whitman tried to get rid of Lewis by persuading some late-passing wagons to take him on down the Columbia. Lewis was gone a few days; then, his new companions having cast him off, he returned to Waiilatpu.

Catherine described the setting to which Lewis came back: "It was now late in the season, and the weather was very inclement. Dr. Whitman's family were all sick. The Indians all had the measles, and owing to their manner of living, dying by the dozen. I have seen from five to six buried daily." Lewis was quick to realize he could turn the epidemic to his own advantage. Should he succeed in driving Whitman off, or having him killed, there would be a rich plantation for the plundering, besides revenge for being pushed around. "The field was well opened for creating trouble, and Joe Lewis improved the opportunity offered."[153]

Lewis played his game by going among the Indians and pointing out to their fear-crazed minds that those Indians whom Whitman treated were dying swiftly. He asked them if they had noticed that the children in the Whitman household were recovering from the measles. This meant, he assured his listen-

Cayuse mat lodges. Sometimes reaching 200 feet in length, the lodges held a number of families, each having its own fire. (Courtesy National Park Serv.)

ers, that Whitman was giving medicine to the whites but was spreading poison among the Indians. He added that he had overheard Whitman plotting to kill off the whole tribe so that he could take its lands for his own purposes.[154] Their people were dying, Whitman's were living. The Cayuses believed Lewis, and the more desperate began planning a way to kill the *tewat*.

Mention must be made too of a shadowy figure who also has been named as being one of the plotters. This was Nicholas Finley, a half-breed living in a lodge within sight of the mission and married to a Cayuse woman. Finley's exact role is not described by any of the survivors of that fall, except that his lodge was said to have served as a headquarters for the ringleaders and their followers. This may well have been true and it may be that Finley was at least sympathetic with the Cayuses; but the lack of evidence strongly suggests he was not a leader of the discontented and he was probably not an active participant in the events to follow. Mary Saunders, the wife of Judge L. W. Saunders and one of the few surviving adults to write about the massacre, said that Finley was sympathetic with the Cayuses. But, from her account, it would seem that Finley's own survival was based partly on his being an ex-employee of the Hudson's Bay Company and partly because he cooperated just enough to stay alive. His concern for Whitman was outweighed by his concern for himself.[155]

Through the cold damp days of November, Whitman was an exhausted, harried man. Day and night he rode among the Indian lodges treating the sick. He had to deal with the hundreds of immigrants, treat their sick, sell or give them supplies. He tried to keep an eye open for capable upright men in the trains whom he could employ for the winter. Then there was the sickness in his own family, nearly all of whom had the measles or other varied diseases. When he could squeeze in a minute or two here and there, a multitude of other tasks awaited his care, such as overseeing the beginning of a new school term with a new teacher, or consulting with Henry Spalding who had brought his daughter, Eliza, down from Lapwai for the fall term. Worriedly, Narcissa watched her husband tear himself apart with concern and physical exhaustion. Fearfully, she remained silent and served as confidant, nurse, and mother to her sick brood.

There were now over 70 people at the mission. Outside the Whitmans' family and the school boarders, most of them were newly-arrived immigrants whom Whitman had hired. Besides Marcus and Narcissa and the ten children present — Perrin had gone to the Dalles to help the rehired Alanson Hinman operate the newly-acquired mission — were three boarders, Eliza Spalding and the two halfbreed sons of a Hudson's Bay employee, David Manson. Andrew Rodgers was still at the mission but had been relieved of his teaching duties in order to concentrate on his ministerial studies. To replace him, Whitman had hired Judge L. W. Saunders. With Saunders were his wife and four children.[156]

Grist mill ruins, Whitman mission, as uncovered by archeologists. (Courtesy National Park Serv.)

For several years Whitman had been working at getting a good sawmill set up in the foothills of the Blues. The machinery had arrived from the East and he had built two small cabins at the site. This winter he hoped to get enough lumber sawed to replace all the sod roofs on the mission buildings with boards. To operate the mill he hired two men, Joseph Smith from Illinois and Elam Young from Missouri, who with their families made a total of twelve living at the sawmill. Elam Young's three sons, ranging from 19 to 24, were already men.

To build the gristmill and to do the necessary carpentry work, including an addition to the main house as well as the new roofs, Whitman had brought Josiah Osborn and his family up from the Willamette. They had been emigrants in 1845, the year after the Sagers, and had been in the party that discovered Henry Sager's grave torn open and the bones scattered over the ground. Besides Osborn and his pregnant wife, there were two girls, Salvijane and Nancy, and a small boy.

William Marsh, a widower trying to care for both a daughter and a grandson, was hired to operate the mill. This gristmill was one of the more important pieces of equipment at the mission. Actually, it was the third and largest mill that Waiilatpu had had over the years. But even its 40-inch stones were overworked in supplying flour and meal to the mission, the immigrants, and the Indians. This fall Whitman was assembling the equipment for an even larger mill.

Besides Joseph Stanfield, two other bachelors had stopped that fall, Jacob Hoffman and Isaac Gilliland. Gilliland, from Long Island, had been a driver for Judge Saunders, but another of his skills was tailoring. Whitman promptly put him to work making the doctor a Sunday suit.

With all this manpower around, Marcus saw he would have to employ a cook. He found her in the person of a widow, Rebecca Hays, who brought with her two children.[157] To round out the mission help were three families having five children each: Peter Hall and wife, W. D. and Mrs. Canfield, and Nathan and Mrs. Kimball.

There were three young people whom Whitman took in because of illness among them: Amos Sales and Lorinda and Crocket Bewley. Sales and Lorinda were sick upon arrival, and Crocket soon joined their ranks. Mrs. Whitman had hopes that Lorinda would be of help around the house once she recovered, especially in teaching the girls a little about manners and female refinements.[158]

Even with Finley and Lewis living with the Cayuses, and the Young and Smith families up at the sawmill cabins, the mission was filled to overflowing. The Whitman family and the school boarders lived in the mission house. This large T-shaped, adobe building was a comfortable, well-built structure that Narcissa had taken great pride in furnishing and painting with her limited resources. But now, with 23 people living in it, conditions were somewhat like that of the terribly crowded winter of 1838 when the reinforcements had piled into the tiny first house. Still, Marcus and Narcissa now had their own bedroom to themselves. Except for three very sick girls, Louise Sager, Helen Mar Meek, and Mary Ann Bridger, who were kept in the living room, the rest of the children made their beds in the attic over the main part of the house.

The Indian Room had been turned over to the Osborn family. There Mrs. Osborn lay waiting her fourth child, and near her Salvijane tossed and moaned with the measles fever. An extra bedroom in the single-story wing was given to the two sick men, Sales and Bewley. Mrs. Hays and her son, Henry Clay, were outfitted with a couch in the kitchen. (No one recounted where her other child slept.) Meanwhile, the carpenters hastened to complete an addition to the wing, an addition that was never completed or needed at Waiilatpu.

Four hundred feet to the east was the commodious mansion house that William Gray had built for his bride in the early 1840's. Ever since Gray had left the mission in 1842, Whitman had used this neat, adobe building as a storehouse in the summer and to house immigrants in the winter, so much so that it had come to be known as the Emigrant House. Now, 29 people were packed into its few rooms. Still more shelter was found by cleaning out the small blacksmith shop that stood halfway between the mission and the emigrant houses. No fewer than eight found space to sleep in its two tiny rooms.

As the gray, cold days of November drew to a close, both Marcus Whitman and the Cayuses knew that a crisis was at hand. Terror and hate were fast overcoming reason and love. But Whitman decided he would remain for the winter at least. He would continue to fulfill the destiny that had brought him to this dark place. The Cayuses made a decision too. If they were to defend and preserve their land, what was left of their people, and their way of life, Marcus Whitman had to die.

Massacre

Mrs. Josiah Osborn gave birth to her fourth child on November 14. It lived but a few hours. At the base of the big hill north of the mission, Marcus Whitman buried the baby in the mission cemetery. But the misery in the Osborns' room, where Salvijane continued to grow weaker from the measles, remained unabated. Ten days later, November 24, she too died.

No one can comfort a mother who has lost her child. Narcissa knew that well, but she murmured her compassion and spoke of God's will and the other expressions the human race has set aside for such unfathomable tragedies. She spoke too of another thought, now the Indians would know of a death among the whites and perhaps their unreasoning attitude towards the doctor and his medicine might lessen. Whitman's people were dying too. But Salvijane's death did not bring about this miracle. Meanwhile, death continued to sweep through the Indian lodges, along with its companions—terror and hate.

On Saturday, November 27, Marcus Whitman and Henry Spalding rode southward 30 miles to the Cayuse lodges on the Umatilla River. There were many sick here as well as on the Walla Walla, and the doctor set about to save what lives he could. Spalding was along for more than just the ride. He planned to preach on the Sabbath, perhaps as a counter-measure to the new Catholic mission. He and Whitman hoped to meet Father Brouillet, the Catholic missionary who had arrived on the Umatilla just that week.

On Sunday afternoon the two men visited the lodge of Stickus, a rather remarkable Cayuse. He was not a Christian but he had proven to be a friend to the Whitmans many times over the past eleven years. He was widely known throughout the white community in Oregon for, year after year, Stickus had met and guided wagon trains across the Blue Mountains. Now he warned Whitman that affairs were very serious and that Whitman's life was once again in danger. He urged the doctor to leave the mission until conditions should change for the better.

Whitman accepted the warnings seriously. Even though it was Sunday and a day of rest, he rode back to Waiilatpu, leaving Spalding, whose horse had fallen on him that day, to rest at Stickus' lodge. That night, as candles flickered in the living room of the mission house, Marcus examined the sick children. Catherine remembered, "Dr. W. got home about ten o'clock that night; he sent my brothers, who were sitting up with the sick children, to bed, telling them that he would sit up himself. After they had retired he examined the patients. When he came to Helen Meek, he thought her to be dying."

Then Marcus asked Narcissa if she would get up from her bed for he wished to talk with her. He told her what Stickus had said that day and he reviewed the dangers that faced the mission. But even now Whitman made no plans to flee. Catherine claimed to have overheard the conversation and that she became quite alarmed. Marcus, guessing she was afraid, came over to her pallet and, "He soothed me with kind words, till I finally fell asleep and slept till morning."[159]

Monday morning came late, enshrouded in fog and cold. It was November 29, 1847. Slowly, the mission came to life. The men began their various tasks; the gristmill rumbled; the sounds of hammers came from the wing of the mission house. Marcus, besides treating the sick, officiated at the funeral of an Indian child whose mother had brought it to the mission for burial. Narcissa had slept little during the night and, exhausted from worry over her children, remained in her bedroom during the morning. Elizabeth Sager brought her breakfast but she would not eat it. Toward noon, feeling slightly refreshed, she got up to help with the dinner. After the noon meal she bathed the girls in the living room.

Some of the men joined Marcus for a few minutes after dinner and he briefly discussed the situation with them. Elizabeth overheard this conversation and now she too became uneasy: "about two hours before the massacre, Mr. Kimball or Mr. King and Mr. Canfield sitting on the settee, I heard Dr. Whitman say, 'If things do not clear up, I shall have to leave in the spring.' "[160]

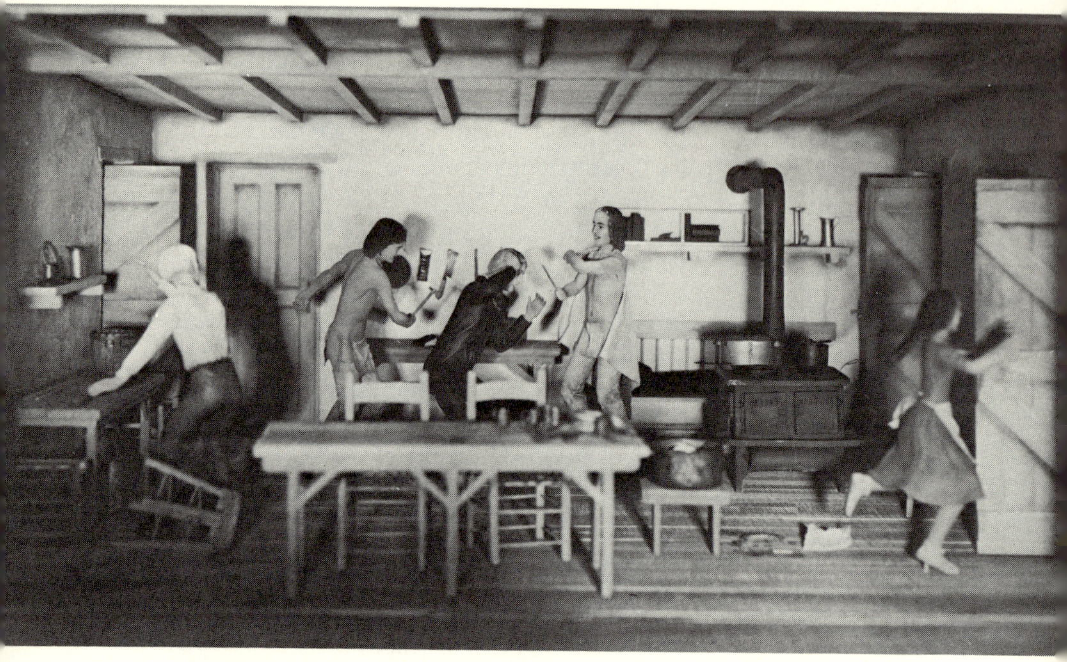

In the diorama above, located in the Whitman Mission visitor center, John Sager, left, is reaching for a pistol to aid Dr. Whitman, whom two Cayuse Indians are attacking. Mary Ann Bridger, daughter of mountain man Jim Bridger, runs off right for help. (Courtesy Whitman Mission NHS.) Below is scene of Whitman's assassination as portrayed in F. F. Victor's *River of the West,* a biographical representation of Joe Meek.

Too weary to visit the lodges, Marcus stayed in the house after dinner. He sat in a corner of the living room, resting and reading, while Narcissa continued her bathing of one sick child after another. John Sager, who was just recovering from the measles, was out in the kitchen preparing twine for new brooms. With him was Mary Ann Bridger. She should have been in school but she too was feeling ill, but well enough to help by washing the noon-time dishes. Francis and Matilda were the only Sagers well enough to attend classes that day and they were in the classroom sizing up the new teacher, Judge Saunders.

Toward two o'clock, two Cayuse leaders, Tiloukaikt and Tomahas, entered the kitchen door. Several Indians had been in and out of the kitchen during the morning and neither John nor Mary Ann had any cause to feel concern about these men. The two Indians walked over to the living room, knocked, and loudly demanded medicine.

Marcus, in the living room, sprang to the door and firmly forbade the Indians to enter. He told them he would get medicine for them but that they would have to wait in the kitchen. He forced the door closed, bolted it, then went to a storage cabinet under the stairway where he kept his medical supplies. Telling Narcissa to lock the door behind him, he went out into the kitchen. Quickly, Narcissa slid the bolt into its slot.

In the kitchen, Marcus gave the medicine to the Indians and explained to them how it was to be used. Tiloukaikt then deliberately provoked the doctor into an argument about it. While Whitman's attention was thus diverted, Tomahas moved unobtrusively behind him. Then, before the helpless eyes of John, Tomahas suddenly drew a tomahawk from his blanket and attacked the doctor from behind. Whitman struggled to save himself but he quickly collapsed from the blows.

Mary Ann Bridger was probably the first to react. She dashed out the kitchen door, ran around the house to the front door of the living room. "She was too much frightened to speak, but when asked if Father was dead, said 'Yes!' "[161] At almost the same time that Mary Ann fled, John jumped from his stool and reached for a pistol lying on a shelf. Before he could grasp it, one of the two Indians raised a musket and fired. John Sager fell to the floor mortally wounded. The boy who had become an

adult overnight back on the Oregon Trail, who had held his sisters and brother together for three years, now lay dying a horribly slow death.

Either the shot that wounded John or another one fired at the same time was the signal for a general attack by the Indians who had carefully spread throughout the yard. Before leaving the kitchen to join in the melee outside, either Tiloukaikt or Tomahas slit open John Sager's throat and stuffed the crimson gap with his shirt.

When he heard the firing, Judge Saunders ran from the schoolroom and dashed across the yard toward his wife in the emigrant house. He did not reach her. Two Indians grabbed him and in a savage fight ended his life with butcher knives.

Jacob Hoffman, with two other men, was butchering a beef that afternoon for the mission tables. Francis Sager, now 14 and fast growing up, had been allowed to help in killing the animal during the noon break from school. When the Indians had gradually sifted in and loitered about the butchering, these men thought that the Cayuses had come to get the entrails and other wastes from the animal as was their custom. But they were wrong in their guess about the Indians' intentions; now Hoffman died, furiously defending himself to the last with an ax.

In the emigrant house, while women and children cowered behind closed doors, the Indians entered the room in which Gilliland was busily sewing Whitman's new suit and attacked the tailor. It was a messy job, but before long Gilliland lay dead. When the shooting started, William Marsh ran from the gristmill where he had been at work. He got only a few steps when he fell mortally wounded by a bullet.

When Judge Saunders ran out of the schoolhouse, the pupils, frightened and bewildered, climbed up into the shallow halfloft above the rafters of the room. Soon after, Joe Lewis came into the schoolroom, found the children in their hiding place, and ordered them down. Unnoticed by Lewis, Francis stayed behind in a corner of the loft. Disappointed that he had not found Francis among the children, Lewis and some of the Indians lined them up apparently with the intention of shooting them en masse. Unable to restrain himself, Francis came out of hiding and went to the group to comfort his sister, Matilda. Some

Tiloukaikt, left and Tomahas, the two Cayuse leaders who attacked Dr. Whitman and John Sager, Nov. 29, 1847. (From the paintings by Paul Kane, courtesy Royal Ontario Museum.)

in the scraggly little line wept, others stood silently, probably too numb to comprehend their situation. Then Lewis came over to Francis and pulled him out of the line. In front of the horrified children, Lewis shot the boy with a pistol. Francis died immediately and did not suffer as others were to do that day.[162]

Two men, Nathan Kimball who was helping Hoffman with the beef, and Andrew Rodgers who was down at the river when the attack started, were wounded in the early minutes of the attack. Both of them were able to run to the mission house, where Narcissa let them into the living room.[163] When the occupants of that room had heard the sound of a gun in the kitchen, they "all started in affright for the outside door."[164] The children ran about hysterically — those being bathed at the moment dashed about without any clothing. The ones too sick to rise cried from their beds. But Narcissa, if she panicked the first few moments, recovered quickly and calmed those with her. The naked children were dressed. Mrs. Hays and Mrs. Hall, who had come in after dinner to help with the sick, now assisted Narcissa in dragging her bleeding, dying husband from the kitchen to a couch in the living room. Marcus was still conscious and was able to answer his wife's question; but he quickly slipped into unconsciousness.[165] The women did not touch John's body as it seemed to them that he was already dead. Again bolting the door, Narcissa set about defending the living room against the attackers. Other than locking the doors, however, there was little she could do. For the moment, the Indians were too busy in their killing of the men to bother with her.

Just after letting in Kimball and Rodgers and binding their wounds, Narcissa looked through the door window and saw Lewis in the south yard. While she was watching him, an Indian standing in the schoolroom doorway saw her and, raising his musket, fired. Mrs. Whitman fell to the floor, blood flowing from an ugly wound in her left breast. She screamed, but the weight of her responsibilities forced her to regain control of herself quickly. Her wound was dressed and calmly now she and Andrew Rodgers planned their next move.[166]

It was probably Rodgers' suggestion that they all take shelter in the attic. Narcissa was helped up the stairs. The two sickest girls, Helen Mar and Louise, were carried up. Only Marcus, who may still have been alive but who was at least unconscious, was left in the living room. No sooner had the others got upstairs when the Indians burst into the mission house, milling about in a frenzy of looting and destruction. They discovered the refugees above them but were kept from rushing the narrow stairs by the barrel of a broken, discarded musket pointing down at them. The Indians did not know it was broken and none of them was willing to climb the stairs. Screaming their obscenities, they tore apart the house and its furnishings.

Finally tiring of their spoiling, they turned their attention again to the stairs. Now they threatened to set fire to the house and to destroy Narcissa and her family if she did not surrender. Tamsucky, an older Cayuse whom the Whitmans had long trusted, now talked with Narcissa and finally convinced her that the house would be burned and that she must come down. Gathering her courage and strength, she slowly came down the stairs, blood-stained bandages pointing out her pain. Behind her came Rodgers, Rebecca Hays, and Mrs. Hall. The children and Kimball stayed behind, waiting and watching to see how much faith to place in the Cayuses' words.

At the foot of the stairs, Narcissa caught a glimpse of Marcus who now lay dead. The attackers had mutilated his face while destroying the living room. The sight of his body drained all the strength from Narcissa. She collapsed and Rodgers lifted her limp body on to the settee. Lewis picked up one end of the couch and ordered Rodgers to take the other. They carried Narcissa through the room, past the blood-soaked body of John in the kitchen, and out through the north door into the yard.

Once outside the door, Lewis dropped his end of the settee and stepped quickly away. Indians standing there raised their guns and fired at Narcissa and Rodgers. Soon, the woman who had tried so hard for so long to do good in this wild country, lay dead. It is said that an Indian, maddened beyond control, grabbed her hair, raised her head, and again and again whipped the dead face with his riding quirt. Andrew Rodgers lay fatally wounded, but to the enjoyment of his attackers he struggled in the mud, suffering a lingering death that did not finally release him from pain until far into the night.

Kimball and the children remained in the attic uncertain

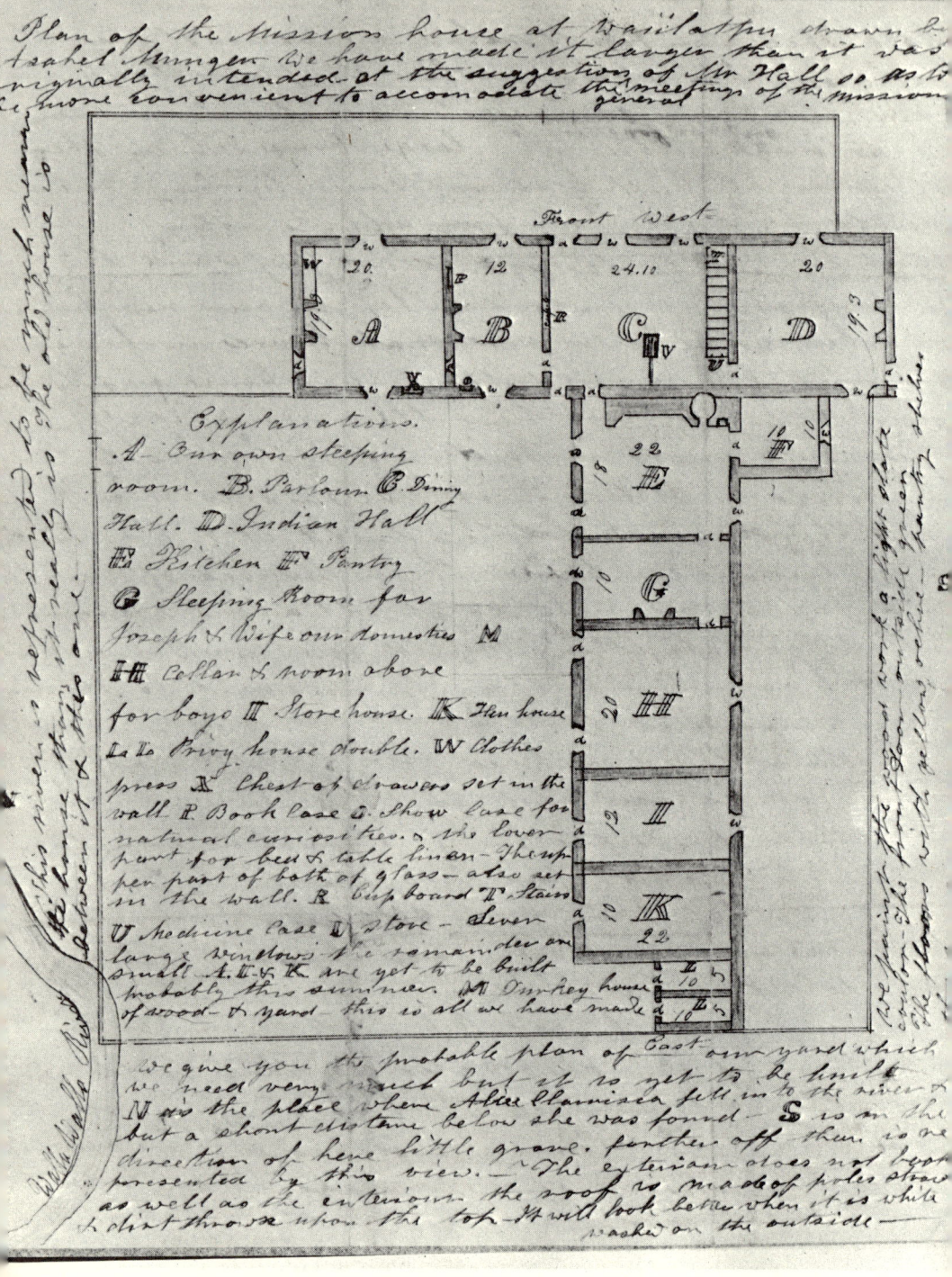

Narcissa Whitman included this plan of the mission house at Waiilatpu in a letter to her father written in May, 1840. During the massacre, John Sager was killed in the kitchen, E. Francis Sager was killed in the yard. Dr. Whitman was wounded in the kitchen, but died in the living room, C. Mrs. Whitman, already wounded, was killed in the yard to the right of E. Classes for the mission children were held in the room H; the loft above was the Sager boys' bedroom. (OHS Collections.)

as to what was happening below, but afraid to come down because of the sounds of gunfire. Through the long night they waited, listening to the slightest sounds with renewed fear. Late in the night, Kimball told Catherine to tear up a bed sheet to make fresh bandages for his wounds.[167] As the night dragged on the sick children cried for water until, near dawn, Kimball decided to go to the river to get water for their fevered throats.

He wrapped himself in a blanket so as to look like an Indian should he be seen. He was not challenged; he reached the river, got the water, and started back to the house. It was then the Indians discovered him. He was shot and killed outright. When the sun came up, it showed Kimball's body sprawled across a fence rail, the bucket lying on the ground below his outstretched fingers. Later that day the Indians allowed the children to move to the emigrant house, where they were cared for by the other survivors of the attack.

The lust to kill had not yet run its course at Waiilatpu. On that second day, Tuesday, one of Elam Young's grown sons, James, rode toward the mission with a wagonload of lumber. The Cayuses stopped him when he was still a mile or so from the mission and gleefully killed the unsuspecting lad on the spot.

Crocket Bewley and Amos Sales were so sick on the day of the attack that they lay helpless in their tiny room. For some unknown reason the Cayuses allowed them to remain unmolested through the day's events. If the two of them had been scared enough to remain silent, they might have lived. But when they learned of the events of the first day, they taunted the Cayuses with dire prophecies of what would happen when the news reached the settlements in the Willamette. One or two more deaths would not bother the Cayuses in the slightest; they hauled Sales and Bewley from their beds and killed them in front of the women and children. This brought the total of dead to 13, twelve men and one woman. With their adopted parents and two brothers dead, the five Sager girls again knew terror and loneliness.

Peter Hall was helping Osborn that fall in building the new addition to the mission house. When the attack had started,

Osborn by chance had been in his room trying to comfort his despondent wife who had not yet been able to rid herself of despair since the loss of two of her children. But Hall was at work that afternoon. When the attack started, he ran. By some good fortune he made his escape successfully and reached Fort Walla Walla where he asked the new factor, William McBean, for help. McBean was no hero and when he learned what was happening at Waiilatpu, he decided to stay as neutral as possible and to give only a minimum of assistance to anyone. But he did give Hall some food and a boat by which to cross the Columbia. At that point, Peter Hall exited from history. Perhaps he drowned in the Columbia; perhaps he was killed by river Indians. History has seen fit to list him missing along with the 13 killed at Waiilatpu.

A few others also attempted flight and, unlike Hall, were successful in reaching safety. One of these was W. D. Canfield, who was the third member of the beef butchering team that afternoon. By sheer luck he managed to hide in the tiny blacksmith shop until darkness fell that terrible Monday. Then he set out on foot for Spalding's mission, 110 miles away. Though he knew only the direction and had never been there before, he reached Lapwai five days later.

A much more desperate escape was made by the Osborn family. When the Indians broke into the living room of the mission house, Josiah had already discovered a loose board in the floor of the Indian room. In the shallow space beneath the floor he hid his wife, two children, and himself. Through the long afternoon they lay cramped while, inches above their heads, the Indians stomped and destroyed. As darkness fell, he could hear the moans of Andrew Rodgers just outside the building as the young man's life now left his body. Finally, when quiet settled over the mission and darkness covered the bloodstains, the Osborns slipped out of hiding and made their way to the river. Following the stream they started walking the 20 miles to Fort Walla Walla.

Mrs. Osborn collapsed before they had gone very far. Her condition offered no hope of immediate recovery, and Josiah regretfully hid her and the children in a tangle of willows at the edge of the river. He hurried on to the fort and persuaded

McBean to give him a horse and some food. Accompanied by a friendly Indian, he returned and, after some difficulty in locating the hiding place, found his family still alive and took them to Fort Walla Walla. This weird adventure took four days altogether, four days in the dank cold of that awful autumn. But through some strength that was not obvious, Mrs. Osborn and the children survived the incident, and they waited at McBean's fort for rescue that would take them to the safety of the Willamette.

The Cayuses were exultant. They had destroyed what they believed had been the source of all their troubles and ills. With the death of the *tewat* and his haughty wife, good times would return and Waiilatpu would be free from wagon wheels and the unfathomable ideas of the whites. The Indians could not know that the Whitmans would become martyrs in the eyes of their countrymen and that a great revenge would be visited upon the tribe.

But for now, the Cayuses sized up their deeds. They allowed the three half-breed boys, David Malin and Manson's two sons, to go to Fort Walla Walla. The rest of the survivors, nearly 50 in number, once the Youngs and the Smiths came down from the sawmill, remained at Waiilatpu as prisoners. Catherine, Elizabeth, Matilda, and Henrietta watched over Louise in a desperate battle to keep her alive. There was no doctor to treat her now and no mother to care for her.

Captivity

For thirty days the survivors of the massacre were held the prisoners of the Cayuses. It was a month of terror and pain for some, and for others it was a time of dazed bewilderment from which emerged a few distinct memories. Elizabeth Sager described it as a time when "We did not know what was to become of us. We lived from minute to minute. As I look back now it seems as if all were demented. I cannot understand why certain things were done, unless it was from the bewilderment of the great shock."[168] So thick was the blanket of discreet silence surrounding the captives in later years, that only hints of "the bewilderment of the great shock" have survived — glimpses that have been discolored by sometimes malicious gossip over the years.

When dawn seeped into the attic of the mission house on Tuesday morning, Catherine Sager knew that Kimball would not return with water. Not knowing if anyone else at the mission was alive besides herself and the girls with her, she froze in terror at the sounds of Indians returning to the house. Shortly, Joe Lewis and several Cayuses came up the stairs and found the children cowered in a corner, the smaller ones crying from fear and thirst. Lewis told them they would not be hurt but would be taken to Fort Walla Walla as soon as a wagon was hitched. He probably meant what he was saying for at this point the Cayuses had not planned anything beyond the killing itself. It would not be long however before the Indians and the captives would both realize that for the time being no one was to be freed.

The Indians who came up the stairs with Lewis asked Catherine why the children were crying. Catherine answered that they were hungry and thirsty. Somewhat to her surprise, yesterday's killers now acted with some concern and brought food and water to the attic. But it was only a gesture, and when the children asked for more water the Indians refused. Catherine

[104]

felt her confidence returning and, when the water was denied, put on her shoes and went to the river herself. "As I was returning," she recalled, "there were some Indians sitting on the fence. One of them drew a gun on me. I walked along expecting to be shot; but he turned the gun and shot it off, and laughed to see me hump."[169]

She got back to the house, which the Indians had temporarily deserted. She brought the girls who could walk downstairs, and the children wandered about the living room gazing at the destruction: broken furniture, strewn feathers and ashes, matted straw and blood, all in one indescribable mess. Whitman's body still lay where it had been left the afternoon before, but someone had covered it. "We went down, and raising the cover from Father's face beheld a sight we will never forget. His face was cut literally to pieces."[170]

They also saw the bodies of John and Francis. But even these bloody corpses did not cause Catherine to falter. About this time Joseph Stanfield came to the house and told her there were women and children at the emigrant house and that she should go there.[171] Catherine returned to the attic and, with the help of Elizabeth and Mary Ann, managed to get Louise down the narrow stairs. Indian women had come into the house meanwhile and were rummaging through the living room looking for loot their husbands had not destroyed the day before. On seeing the girls, the women gave them some clothing they had collected. But none offered to help move Helen Mar, who was now left in the house crying hysterically as Catherine led her sisters across the yard.

Those in the emigrant house greeted Catherine and her sisters with tears. They had not known that anyone with the Whitmans had lived through the attack. The security of friends at last overwhelmed Catherine. All the strain finally caught up with her. Only now did she let herself go and faint. When she revived, she remembered that Helen Mar was still in the mission house. She persuaded some of the group to accompany her back to get the child. Of the thirteen who together had made the Whitman family, only seven were alive at Waiilatpu. Marcus and Narcissa, John, and Francis were dead. Perrin, at the Dalles, was not yet aware of what had taken place at the mission. David

Father J.B.A. Brouillet buried victims of the massacre, including John and Francis Sager. *(Oregon Native Son.)*

Malin had already gone to Fort Walla Walla. The survivors at Waiilatpu, dazed and bewildered, moved almost automatically, realizing vaguely that the dead had to be buried.

On Wednesday morning, Father J. B. A. Brouillet, the new Catholic priest on the Umatilla River, rode toward Waiilatpu in haste and concern. He had promised Whitman to visit him this day, but now he had heard of the terrible event. Steeling himself for the worst, he was still shocked at the sight of the bloodied bodies strewn about. Joseph Stanfield had already dug a mass grave near the mission cemetery and was getting ready to gather the bodies to prepare for burial as best he could. He quickly described to Brouillet the events of the past two days, then took the priest to the emigrant house to comfort the survivors.

Other than Stanfield, the entire group of captives was Protestant. Most of them had never had any dealings with a priest of the Catholic Church. The mission children, particularly, had been taught to think of a priest as an agent of the devil, or worse. Now they had their strange meeting. Elizabeth Sager later wrote, unkindly but truthfully, that she was more afraid of Brouillet than she had been of the Indians at the height of the attack.[172]

The women had been preparing shrouding for the dead when Brouillet arrived. He told them to finish their preparations and when all was ready he would perform the burial service. Thus the great irony came about that Marcus Whitman, to whom the arrival of the Catholics had caused so much concern, was now buried by a priest of that faith. Neither Henry Spalding nor the Sager girls, who were to come under his nativist philosophy, were ever to forgive the Catholic Church for this. But Brouillet had no choice. Horrified by the slaughter, he sadly rendered "to those unfortunate victims the last service in my power to offer them."[173]

As soon as the funeral was over, Brouillet left Waiilatpu intent on returning to his own station. Before he had ridden far he met Henry Spalding who had not yet heard of the attack. Brouillet told him of the massacre and urged Spalding not to go to the mission where surely he too would die. Henry heeded the priest and made a wide detour around Waiilatpu and hastened to Lapwai fearful that his own family might already be dead.

Meanwhile, his daughter, Eliza, was very much alive at Waiilatpu. There were five rooms in the emigrant house, and the survivors divided themselves so that about two families occupied each room. Joseph Smith, Elam Young, his sons Daniel and John, and Joseph Stanfield were the only mission men left. The Indians put Smith and Young to work at the gristmill, grinding wheat and corn for the tribe. Because neither of the two men could speak the Indian language, Eliza Spalding was also sent to the mill each day to act as an interpreter. But Eliza found it a lonely, fearful way to spend her time and she persuaded Elizabeth to go with her. "It was so cold in the mill that we dug a hole in a strawstack nearby and put a blanket in front of it for a door. Eliza and I crawled in there where we could be out of the wind. When the Indians wanted Eliza they would raise the blanket and tell her to come on out and talk for them."[174]

Each day the rougher element among the Indians would arrive at the emigrant house — their women rarely accompanying them — bringing with them food which the captives then had to prepare, and cloth for the women to sew into shirts.

These men lounged about all day and far into the night. When the hostages nervously made up their beds, the Indians would promptly lie down on them, conversing, smoking, and acting their roles of lords and masters. It was usually midnight before they would depart for their lodges.

In those first days, the Indians held two councils that all the captives were forced to attend, even three-year-old Henrietta. At the first meeting the Cayuses announced that the prisoners would be held all winter but would be freed when spring came. If, however, whites from the Willamette should attack, then all the captives would be killed. This was sobering news; however, the second council brought greater consternation. This time, the prisoners heard that the young women among them would be taken as wives by the leading members of the tribe.[175]

The record is not clear, purposefully so it would seem, as to how many of the widows and teen-age girls were violated during the month. It was certainly not many. Less than a dozen could have been considered eligible, and some of these were probably safe in that they were no longer young enough to attract much attention. However, for all the women, the four weeks of captivity were a trying time. It was still an age when rape was "a fate worse than death," and the women spent many an hour devising and carrying out ruses and delaying tactics in self-protection. From the Indians' point of view, the white women's attitude was curious if not incomprehensible. Since time immemorial it had been the privilege of the captor to seduce the women he had taken. From the captives' point of view there "never before appeared upon the annals of American history where female captives were treated with like brutality." The complete story of this period of captivity will never be known. Catherine Sager, in the most detailed account of this month, wrote: "I have endeavored to present them in such a manner as to spare the feelings of those concerned. For this reason I have not related many things that would be interesting."[176]

Surely the most tragic case involved 19-year-old Lorinda Bewley. Just before her brother was killed, an Indian entered the room where she was still lying sick in bed. He began to fondle her, but she fought him off. In a fury, he dragged her outdoors and tried to put her on his horse. She continued to fight

Five Crows, Cayuse chief, as sketched by Gustav Sohon in 1855.

him but, while she succeeded in staying off the horse, she only enraged the Indian further. He threw her to the ground and raped her in front of the astonished eyes of the rest of the captives. His passions finally dying, he let her go. The women surrounded her, brought her into the house, and treated her as best they could. But they knew hardly what to do; this was quite beyond their experience.[177]

A few days later, Five Crows, the only Cayuse to have been baptized by the missionaries, came up to Waiilatpu and took Lorinda Bewley back to his lodge on the Umatilla. There he kept her captive and forced her into sexual relations. Those still at Waiilatpu were certain they would not see Lorinda alive again.[178]

If these deeds aroused the anger of the white settlements when they became known, an even more questionable action by one of the white captives was quietly ignored — except by one or two of the captives. When the Indians made known their desires for women, Joseph Smith did some thinking. He was one of the few men left. While the Indians needed him for the moment to grind corn, his life might be more secure if his relations were strengthened with them. Chief Tiloukaikt's son, whom the missionaries had named Edward, was looking with interest at Smith's daughter, Mary. Smith talked to the girl and found that she was not wholly repelled by the stalwart young Indian. A courtship of sorts followed, then Edward took Mary to bed. The only other case mentioned by the survivors by name was that of Susan Kimball, whose father had died trying to get water for the sick children on that first night. An Indian called Francis took Susan as his woman.[179]

The deaths of Bewley and Sales and the rape of Lorinda Bewley were not all the tragedies witnessed at Waiilatpu during Sunday, December 5. Louise Sager had been dangerously ill since before the massacre, and even had Marcus Whitman lived he may well not have been able to save her life. Sunday afternoon an exhausted Catherine had lain down next to her sister to get some much-needed sleep. When she awoke, Lorinda Bewley was in the room. In answer to Catherine's questions about Louise, Lorinda said the child was better and that she had eaten her supper, then fallen asleep. "I still sat looking at my sister," said Catherine, "Her hands were thrown over head, and she seemed to be in a sound slumber. Miss B. remarked, 'How nicely L. sleeps!' Laying my hand on her face, I found it icy cold. I lay my ear to her mouth, but the breath was gone. I said, 'Louise is dead!' " Henry Sager's seven were now but four.

Daniel Young, the 21-year-old son of Elam, made a coffin for her tiny body and the next day Joseph Stanfield dug a grave in the waving rye grass north of the mission. Three days later Helen Mar Meek died. She was buried next to Louise Sager. Perhaps she too could not have been saved even if the doctor were there. Her father, Joseph Meek, was never to forgive the Cayuses when he learned of her death.

On December 9, just before retiring, Mary Walker at Tshimakain sat at a table making her daily entry in her diary. Heavy with child and dejected in mind she picked up her pen: "We were hoping to have Dr. Whitman to supper with us tonight. But about sunset Old Solomon arrived bringing the sad intelligence that Dr. & Mrs. Whitman, Mr. Rogers, John and Francis Sager & others have been murdered by the Indians." This time, Dr. Whitman would not even be able to send his advice to let nature take its course.[181] At the same time, Henry Spalding was back with his family in the Nez Percé country. He had had a harrowing journey home, especially after his horse had run away from him. When Henry had reached the Lapwai valley he had found his family safe at the home of his only white neighbor, a "heathen" and a bitter foe, William Craig. The Spaldings soon learned from two trusted Nez Percés that Eliza was still alive and well at Waiilatpu, but the Cayuses had refused to let her return to Lapwai. The captivity of his daughter, the deaths of the Whitmans, and his own dangerously narrow escape from the Cayuses resulted in a great strain on Henry's already delicate nerves, a strain from which he was never fully to recover.

But his daughter was doing as well as anyone had a right to expect when one is a captive. Her command of the Indian tongue and her tender age made her too valuable a tool for the Indians to harm. Accompanied by her close friend Elizabeth, she was kept busy at interpreting and had little time to worry about the future. And in being so occupied, she kept Elizabeth's spirits up also. Perhaps the morale of the two girls was not terribly high but it was somewhere above despair.

Catherine found herself with little time to sorrow over Louise and Helen Mar. However, the things that occupied her mind were far different than those that concerned Elizabeth and Eliza. At twelve, Catherine was on the verge of womanhood, a fact that had not escaped the attention of her Indian captors. The first to demand her affections was Edward, the son of Tiloukaikt. This, of course, was before he "married" Mary Smith.

At first Catherine did not object to Edward's curiously gentlemanly advances. He asked her to teach him English, which she agreed to do. Using one of Dr. Whitman's Bibles as a textbook, Catherine had her pupil repeat each word after her, "One day as we sat at our studies he gave me a cotton handkerchief, telling me to wear it at all the time [*sic*] on my head or neck, and the other Indians would never hurt me, for they would know that I was his girl."[182]

But it was not long before Edward overstepped the imaginary line that Catherine had drawn about herself. He told her he knew she was young but he would like to have her for a wife anyway. Catherine was alarmed and tried to divert his attentions by suggesting that he ask Mary Smith if that was what he wanted. Thus, for the moment, Joseph Smith and Catherine Sager were unwittingly allies. Edward did as Catherine suggested, and he was not rebuffed by Mary.

Catherine soon regretted her action. If Edward had been bold, he was at least reasonable. Without his handkerchief to protect her, Catherine soon became the desire of another Indian: "One evening I was sitting by the fire in Mrs. Hall's room," she wrote, "when Istulest came in and gathered me by the arm and dragged me into our room, which was empty except for the presence of the sleeping children." She continued, "He set a chair and told me to sit down. He then went on to talk to me about marrying one of his friends. The friend soon made an appearance, and I had to sit all the evening to his love speeches." One of the mission people came in at an opportune moment and told the Indians not to take Catherine away, "They said they did not intend to."[183]

The two Indians then forced Catherine, who was wrapped in a blanket, to lie on the bed with the sleeping children: "They made me get into it on the back side. The Indian then crowded in next the wall. I went to bed with my shoes on. I applied these to his shins till he cried out lustily. The other Indian now left."[184]

Nothing more serious happened to Catherine that night. The next day the adult prisoners tried to think of some scheme by which she could be protected from her would-be lover. Stanfield suggested that she sleep in the strawstack down by the gristmill. Someone else thought she should move to Finley's lodge and that one of the Young boys should go with her as a guard. Catherine herself gave serious thought to jumping into the millpond should the would-be seducer appear again. Finally, Elam Young thought of the simple scheme of hiding Catherine in the bedding early in the evening and then having others sit in front of the pile of quilts. This plan was tried that night and it worked. Catherine's pursuer came and searched the house, but he failed to find her and left in an ugly, defeated mood.[185]

A few nights later, Catherine was asleep in her own bed when "I became conscious of some one pulling me by the arm. I awoke and found it to be mine enemy. He wanted me to sit by the fire to talk with him. This I refused to do, he undertook to make me. I called to the Indians till I found it no use. He threatened to whip me if I did not do as he wished. I lost all fear of him in my desperation and fought him with all my might, using my teeth freely." They wrestled, but Catherine would not surrender, and her screams finally brought the mission men to her aid. Her attacker left never to come back. Later, the Indians considered Catherine to be an extraordinarily brave girl for having got the best of a warrior.[186] This was the last time Catherine was bothered by any of the men. But it left a memory forever sharply etched in her mind. Just as her brother John had grown up overnight three years earlier, she too now became an adult in mind. The Indians were only one of her problems, she was now the head of the family as well.

Just as the joy of youth so quickly overcame adversity on the Oregon Trail three years earlier, so it did again at Waiilatpu. True, it was no time to laugh, but laugh the children did when they saw an Indian warrior riding through the mission yard using the large map of the world from the schoolroom as his saddle.[187]

When the younger Indians were hanging about the mission house, night after night, keeping the captives awake and ever watchful for an incident, one of the captives suggested the idea of getting a few of the older, quieter Indians to stay with them in the evenings to ward off the unwanted attentions of the younger ones. For a while this scheme worked out very well. The women paid off their protectors by serving sweets or sewing up a shirt for them. One of the more trusted of these "guards" was an elderly respected Indian named Beardy. Either on Christmas Day or a few days before, Mrs. Saunders disclosed that she had hidden away some white flour and some dried peaches that she had brought all the way from the East.[188] With these, she made a large number of peach pies. Beardy had been kind to the captives and she offered a large portion of the pies to him, "He had eaten heartily through the day, and at night he ate very heartily of the pies."

Later that night, Beardy awoke sick unto death. He threw up the pies and, convinced he was losing blood rather than peaches, cried aloud that the captives had poisoned him and that he was dying. The next morning, still alive, to his surprise, Beardy found the strength to harangue his friends into attacking the emigrant house and killing all the captives. It took a great deal of persuasion and diplomacy to convince Beardy that he was merely the victim of his own greed. Had it not been for the timely arrival of an Indian woman from Fort Hall, whose husband was the white employee of the Hudson's Bay Company, and who now served as a mediator between the two parties, Beardy and his associates might well have brought the period of captivity to a tragic close. As Catherine put it, "He was very much ashamed of himself," when he found out his error.[189]

Unknown to the captives, even before the Beardy incident, three boats had arrived at Fort Walla Walla on December 19. Aboard one of them was the survivors' chief hope of salvation, Peter Skene Ogden of the Hudson's Bay Company from Fort Vancouver.

"A Free People"

As soon as William McBean heard about the massacre from Peter Hall and Josiah Osborn, he sent a messenger to Fort Vancouver to inform the Board of Management, the successor to the former Chief Factor, Dr. McLoughlin. The Board included James Douglas and Peter Skene Ogden.[190] The messenger obeyed his instructions faithfully and while enroute to Fort Vancouver told no one he met about the attack, leaving even Perrin Whitman at the Dalles ignorant of the event. Immediately upon getting the news, the Hudson's Bay Company prepared to send an expedition to the interior to obtain the release of the prisoners.

The massacre and the captivity were an American affair, one in which the Hudson's Bay Company officials might not be expected to wish involvement. However, just as it had done so much to assist the American Board missions to maintain themselves during the past eleven years, the Company now did everything it could to effect the release of the captives. For generations it had learned, sometimes painfully, how to get along with the multitude of tribes over much of the northern half of the continent. Ever since it had entered the Oregon Country in the 1820's, it had carefully developed its relations with most of the tribes from Alaska to California. If the Cayuses were to trust any white men in the delicate field of negotiations, it would be the Company officials who would succeed, not the impatient American settlers. The whites in the Willamette Valley would rise to anger and seek revenge when the news became common. A brash or vengeful man would more likely precipitate the captives' death than their freedom.

Even the Cayuses realized they could expect an armed force from the lower Columbia.[191] This was why they had decided to keep the survivors as hostages, and this is why they made use of the priests to transmit their grievances and feelers for negotiations to the lower country. When the news of the massacre did spread through the countryside, each group prepared for its assumed role: the Hudson's Bay Company to secure the prisoners' freedom; the Americans to revenge the deaths; the Indians to salvage as much as possible from their crisis.

Peter Skene Ogden had visited the Columbia River missions several times over the years and had hosted Marcus Whitman at Fort Vancouver when the doctor was down on his trips for supplies. He may not have expected the missions to have unqualified results in their work, but he had developed a respect for Whitman and his associates and knew them to be dedicated people. His small party, aboard three boats, arrived at Fort Walla Walla on December 19. Ogden put out a call for the Cayuses to come to the fort for a council. They accepted his invitation. The prisoners, when they learned of this development from the Indians, cautiously let their hopes rise that rescue might be imminent.[192]

When the council got underway on December 23, Ogden was careful not to put too much pressure on the Indians. He knew the difference between leading and driving and he carefully avoided making any promises he could not keep. He reminded the Cayuses of the Company's long history of good relations with the Indians. Then he came to the issue at hand. He expressed shock at the attack on the missionaries and he emphasized that the Americans of the Willamette would be intensely angry. He refused to promise that he could stay the guns of the Americans, promising only to carry the Cayuses' thoughts to the American authorities. He noted that he was now a foreigner in this country, a British subject, with no other intention in mind than to seek the freedom of the Cayuses' hostages. "I give you only advice," he said, "and promise you nothing, should war be declared against you. The company have nothing to do with your quarrel. If you wish it, on my return I will see what can be done for you; but I do not promise to prevent war. Deliver me the prisoners to return to their friends, and I will pay you a ransom, that is all."[193]

In the end the Indians believed Ogden. When it became clear they would exchange their prisoners for material compensation, the wily trader then settled down to the hard business of bargaining. When the details were worked out, the Cayuses had agreed to exchange all their captives for

    62 blankets, three-point   600 loads of ammunition
    63 shirts, cotton   12 flints
    12 guns   37 pounds of tobacco

So successful was Ogden in his negotiations that twenty miles away, at Waiilatpu, without further prompting, Five Crows suddenly returned Lorinda Bewley to the emigrant house. It was a joyous reunion and there was little sleep in the girls' room that night as Lorinda thrilled them with "a graphic account of her life during her absence."[194]

On December 29, a small caravan moved out from the mission heading westward toward Fort Walla Walla. The 20 miles between the two places would take a full day's travel for oxen under the best of conditions, but now the trail was muddy and the tributaries of the Walla Walla were full to overflowing. Before long, the wagons began to spread farther and farther apart, the heavier loads and the lazier oxen falling behind. In the lead, Joseph Stanfield drove his friend, Rebecca Hays. Also in this strange cargo was the Smith family, including Mary who with some mild regrets had deemed it prudent to leave Edward.[195]

The last wagon was driven by Elam Young. Besides his own family he had Mrs. Saunders and her children, Mary Marsh, Eliza Spalding, and the four Sager girls. It was bitterly cold, one of those forlorn mornings such as are found in the Walla Walla Valley at the height of winter. Fortunately, there was no snow to slow the wagons even more. As the oxen plodded through the mud and wet grass, neither clouds nor cold could dampen the high spirits in the wagons. Still there was the unspoken fear that the Cayuses would change their minds and not let the prisoners reach the fort.[196] The Indians realized that the Americans would sooner or later attack them and hostages would be valuable when that time came. In case any of the Cayuses changed their minds, two leaders, the reliable Stickus and an abashed Beardy, rode escort to the wagons. Should an incident arise they might be able to cool the hotter tempers of uneasy Indians.

Ft. Walla Walla, Hudson's Bay post at confluence of Walla Walla and Columbia rivers. (John Mix Stanley sketch, 1853. Courtesy Penrose Memorial Library, Whitman College.)

At last, on the ridge of a long gentle hill, at the edge of the wind-swept desert bordering the Columbia, the survivors were able to make out the shadow of Fort Walla Walla far below them. Darkness was fast coming on and even the most jaded of the oxen was whipped into a faster step. Then came the joyous arrival. The Sagers' wagon was an hour behind Stanfield's in reaching the gate. Ogden came out to greet this last wagon and led the survivors into the living quarters of William McBean.

Fort Walla Walla was not a very substantial structure in 1847. Located on the barren east bank of the Columbia just a short distance above the mouth of the Walla Walla, it was little more than a compound enclosed with a palisade of logs. A determined war party could quite easily have gained entry had it a mind to do so. Normally the complement consisted of the factor, five or six employees, and their wives and children, such as the Manson boys. The Ogden party and the more than 50 survivors crowded the fort to the maximum. The newcomers were first taken to the McBean living room where, seated before a blazing fireplace, they enjoyed a hot supper. As soon as the meal was over, they were led to their rooms, in which they were instructed to remain and to open their doors to no one.[197] Ogden was not taking chances of a muddle-minded Indian slipping inside intent on last-minute revenge.

The in-gathering was not yet complete. The anxious party had to wait two long days for the arrival of Henry Spalding and his family from Lapwai. Word had been sent to Spalding to bring his people out, but it would take time to make the trip of more than 150 miles. Through the long hours of the 30th and the 31st, the survivors kept to their rooms. A passer-by on the Columbia might have thought the fort deserted, or nearly so. Inside, the whites lived uneasily. Outside, the Indians pondered if they had done the right thing. There was a slight scare on Friday night. It was not fully explained to the girls. "Catherine, Elizabeth, and Mary Smith, along with several others, were in Mrs. McBain's room when Mr. McBain came in and locked the doors and darkened the windows, telling them not, under any circumstances, to let the Indians see them, and to be very careful of what they said, as 'the very walls have ears.' "[198]

New Year's morning found the fort still in a state of quiet tension. However the mood changed to excitement when the Spaldings arrived from Lapwai. They had been escorted down by 50 Nez Percés who were determined that Henry should not come to harm before he was out of their country. They were not desirous of becoming involved in the troubles that would surely engulf their Cayuse neighbors. Besides Henry and Eliza there were their three youngest children, a young immigrant woman named Mary Johnson who had been employed to help Eliza at the mission, a hired man named Jackson, and Mrs. Spalding's brother, Horace Hart, who had migrated to Oregon just the year before. Spalding had been able to bring out very little of his property, nothing other than a few personal possessions and some livestock. The rest of the material evidence of his eleven years of work remained at Lapwai, abandoned to the pillages of time and Indians. At Fort Walla Walla the Spaldings were reunited with Eliza, their joy lessened by their shock at seeing the effects of captivity in her face and body.

At daybreak the next morning, Sunday, January 2, 1848, the three bateaux pushed out from the river bank and headed down-

Wascopam, the Methodist mission at the Dalles. Massacre survivors passed here on their way to freedom in January, 1848, a year before Wm. H. Tappan made this painting. (OHS Collections)

stream. McBean and his men waved from the shore. The sobs of David Malin, who was left behind, haunted the scene.[199] Snow fell silently, and soon Fort Walla Walla disappeared. The boats glided through the black water, into the big bend of Wallula Gap. High on the basaltic cliffs to their left, the travelers could glimpse the Rocks of the Cayuse Girls, the two great molar-like blocks of basalt that had been the landmark for Fort Walla Walla and the Whitman mission.[200] Then they too disappeared, and the curent carried the boats westward between the great cliffs toward new hopes.

Nancy Osborn, once again with the Sager girls, described the journey down the river: "The boats had to be unloaded at nights and drawn ashore to keep them from freezing fast in the ice. You can imagine something of the trip. When we arrived at the Dalles we met some of the volunteers, for there were no regular soldiers on this coast then. We met more at the Cascades. They helped us make a five-mile portage. The boats had to be carried on men's shoulders. Every child who could walk and carry a bundle had to do so. Not much of a pleasure trip, you will say, but there was gladness in our hearts."[201]

When they passed the Dalles, the Sager girls did not get to see Perrin Whitman. On his way upstream, Ogden had urged the young Whitman and Hinman to leave Wascopam and to go below to the Willamette until matters were more settled. Even then, Perrin was preparing to return to Waiilatpu with the militia.

Once beyond the Dalles, in the great gorge of the Columbia, the survivors knew they were at last safe. The Sagers made a new friend on the trip, an exciting young man who was an artist, John Mix Stanley. He had arrived at Tshimakain early in November on an Indian-painting expedition. There he had painted the portraits of Elkanah Walker and his pretty daughter, Abigail, with whom Catherine had played on her visit the past summer. Toward the end of November, Stanley had left Tshimakain on his way to visit the Whitmans. When he was just a few miles from the mission he learned of the massacre through his guide, Solomon, from a passing Indian. Solomon had led him to Fort Walla Walla then hastened back to Tshimakain to tell Mary Walker the dreadful news. Along with the Osborns, Stanley

Peter Skene Ogden, Hudson's Bay Co. factor who negotiated release of captives. (OHS Collections.)

had waited at the fort for a means of going down the Columbia.

He was fascinated with the disaster that had just occurred and, although he had apparently seen neither the Whitmans nor the mission, he prepared sketches of the attack based on the survivors' descriptions.[202] He took a great liking to the four Sagers, whose young lives had already absorbed so much tragedy. Elizabeth Sager told her own daughter in later years that she did not think she would have reached Fort Vancouver had it not been for Stanley's concern and care. "When they went ashore at night, Stanley would unbuckle his holsters and hand them to Catherine. He called her his 'armor bearer.' Then he would take little Henrietta in his arms and carry her to the encampment, wrap the children up, seat them near the fire and see that they had something to eat."[203]

The trip down the Columbia took four days. On Friday afternoon, January 6, the oarsmen turned the bateaux toward the jetty at Fort Vancouver, the post that Narcissa Whitman had once called "the New York of the Pacific Ocean."[204] Ogden's associate, James Douglas, welcomed the survivors and offered them the famous hospitality of the Hudson's Bay Company for the next few days. Stanley continued to see the children each day and as a farewell present gave them gifts of dress material. These children, who had few possessions other than the clothes they wore, did not forget the kindness.

Douglas and his wife discussed the future of the four Sagers with Henry Spalding, who seemed to be the person most responsible for their welfare now. Mrs. Douglas suddenly announced to Spalding that she would like to keep Elizabeth with her. Another of the fort ladies spoke up and asked if she could take in Catherine and Henrietta. But Henry Spalding would hear of no such arrangement. Coldly he noted that the Sager girls were Presbyterians and he could not allow them to live in a Catholic environment.[205] Although Henry was quite mistaken, since neither Ogden nor Douglas were Catholic, Ogden supported Henry's refusal to give up the girls. Ogden had rescued them and had brought them this far. On Monday he was going to deliver all of them to the American governor, across the river. Then, and only then, they could go where they wished.[206]

On Monday, with mounting excitement, the whole party, which now neared 100 in number, counting the oarsmen, rowed across the Columbia to where the city of Portland now stands. There were already a few log cabins, "two white houses," and a wharf to mark the future metropolis. When the boats neared the wharf, the occupants could distinguish a group of people waiting their arrival. First and foremost stood Governor George Abernethy, who had once been a missionary himself. With him was the Sagers' old friend and guardian, Uncle Billy Shaw. Near Shaw stood Colonel Gilliam who had tried to lead Henry Sager to Oregon. Gilliam was now a "general" and in command of the Oregon Volunteers, a number of whom were on hand to welcome the survivors.

As the boat touched the dock, a number of volunteers presented arms then fired a salute: "We children were terrified. We crawled under some canvas and tried to hide in the bottom of the boat. We thought they were trying to kill us."[207] Someone explained to the gun-shy children that the firing was in their honor. They crawled out in time to see the Britisher, Peter Skene Ogden, turn over the survivors to the custody of Governor Abernethy. The Hudson's Bay Company had done its part; the survivors were the Americans' problem now. Turning to the group, Ogden bade them farewell: "Now you are a free people. You can go where you please."[208]

This was the end of the common thread that had bound these people to one another. For all of them it had been a long journey. Henry Sager's dream of a voyage to a wondrous future where men would be prosperous, content, and free had started a long time ago. It had been a journey far different than the one that he, and thousands of others, had contemplated in the beginning. It was well for 19th century America and for the westward movement that these wanderers could not see the future while they were still on the eastern shore of the Missouri. But perhaps even dire prophecies would not have stopped them. Death and failure had to come to all men someplace, sometime. Better to have failed in trying anew, better to have died chasing a dream.

Now they parted. Hurt Lorinda Bewley would find marriage and would raise a family. Weak Joseph Smith would disappear into the fabric of the new land's history. Sick Mary Ann Bridger had but a few months to live. Strange Joseph Stanfield would not in his lifetime receive the thanks due him. These and all the others had arrived at last at the Willamette.

Abernethy invited the Spalding family and the four Sagers to stay at his home at Green Point, near Oregon City, until they could find suitable homes.[209] For three years, Henry's and Naomi's wish to keep the children together had been honored, now the promise was at last to be broken. John, Francis, and Louise were dead. The survivors, Catherine, Elizabeth, Matilda, and Henrietta were each to go her own way. From time to time their lives would touch again as the years went on in the Oregon Country.

Interlude

Fifty years later, in 1897, the last of the Sagers and the other living survivors of the massacre would again be at Waiilatpu honoring their dead. Before tracing the remaining lives of the four sisters, it would be appropriate to glance briefly at the aftermath of the massacre. This story has been adequately told in detail in several good studies and one should turn to these histories to know all the story. The surviving Sagers were not directly involved with the events that occurred at Waiilatpu after they left. But even today their presence is very much felt by the visitor who stands a moment at the Great Grave or who wanders among the marked ruins of the mission buildings.

The southern half of the old Oregon Country had become a part of the territory of the United States in 1846, but the Federal Government had still not seen fit to establish a territorial government at the time of the Whitman massacre. Just before his death, Whitman had submitted a letter to the War Department for the second time, recommending that the U.S. Army establish forts along the Oregon Trail and in the Oregon Country. Among the early settlers, others made similar requests. Meanwhile, the provisional government, developed by the settlers themselves, continued to function after a fashion in handling the common concerns.

When the news of the Cayuses' attack on the mission spread through the American settlements of the lower Columbia, the predictable outburst of wrath and desire to take revenge developed. These people had never been interested in saving Indians' souls, only in creating for themselves and their families a security that now seemed in doubt. Although Waiilatpu was 200 miles away, across the Cascade Mountains, every able-bodied man in Oregon felt that the attack was a threat to his own future.

Since there were no federal troops, the provisional legislature appealed to the people for volunteers. Almost immediately a company was formed. This company, untrained, undisciplined, and undaunted, would have been glad to have undertaken the task of defeating the Cayuses by itself. But wiser heads prevailed and the Oregon Volunteers were increased to 500.

Under Gilliam, who was given another chance to show if he could lead, the troops entered the Walla Walla Valley at the end of February. There were several skirmishes as they approached the Whitman mission; but cautiously and skillfully the Indians retreated in front of them. Had the white troops been better trained and more amenable to orders, they might have ended the campaign quickly. But they were not. The Cayuses continued to withdraw without serious casualties, finally crossing the Snake River and disappearing into the mountains to the northeast. The Volunteers made one or two forays across the Snake, and a small force rode to Tshimakain to escort the Walkers and Eellses to Waiilatpu and to the coast. But spring had come and it was time to get the crops planted if the soldiers' families were to eat the following winter. Thus, the Cayuse campaign ended and the majority of the militia returned home. Fifty volunteers stayed at the mission throughout the summer.

When the Volunteers had reached the mission in early March, they had found that the Cayuses had set fire to the mission buildings and had pulled down most of the adobe walls. The soldiers cleaned up some of the rubble and built an adobe wall around the ruins of the mission house. Rebuilding the house enough so that it gave some shelter, they named it Fort Waters after the officer, James Waters, who succeeded Gilliam as commanding officer. Poor Gilliam had not lived long enough to return to the Willamette for a victor's acclaim. In preparing to leave Waiilatpu, he was in the act of pulling a rope from a wagon bed when it caught on a musket trigger. The musket discharged, killing Gilliam instantly. "Thus died an honest, patriotic, and popular man, whose chief fault as an officer was too much zeal and impetuosity in the performance of his duties; whose glory would have been to die in battle."[210]

The Volunteers found the mass grave opened by wolves and the bones scattered along the foot of the hill. Had Stanfield still been there he would have been blamed for digging the grave too shallow. The soldiers dug the hole deeper, gathered the

Joseph L. Meek, whose daughter died at Waiilatpu, and who as sheriff hanged the Cayuse Indians found guilty. (Buchtel & Stolte photo, OHS.)

skeletons (Perrin Whitman was a witness), and placed them in it. To give it protection, they upturned a wagon box over the hole, then covered it all with earth.

The Cayuses had not been defeated, but they were nonetheless shattered as a tribe. Already weakened in numbers by the measles, and now more so by the skirmishes and the flight, they dispersed in small groups along the Bitterroots, a few living with the easternmost Nez Percés, Flatheads, Coeur d'Alenes, and with still other tribes in the buffalo country farther east. After two years of wandering and hardship, the survivors longed to return to the camas meadows, salmon streams, and chinook winds of the Walla Walla Valley. In 1850 five of their men were surrendered to the whites in an effort to make peace; among the five were Tiloukaikt and Tomahas.[211]

These five were arrested and charged with murder. They were tried in Oregon City. But there was never any doubt about the outcome of the trial. Four of them undoubtedly had taken part in the attack; the fifth was possibly innocent; all· were hanged. The hangman was Joe Meek, who took great satisfaction in the act as he thought of the bones of his daughter, Helen Mar, spread through the rye grass at Waiilatpu.

But the Indian-white problems were not solved by the hangings. Indeed, these problems were just beginning. The Cayuses were destroyed as a tribe and would never again be a serious threat in the Pacific Northwest, but for the next generation other Indian wars involving larger tribes were to plague the area.

At the same time the Oregon Volunteers marched to Waiilatpu, both Governor Abernethy and the provisional legislature sent emissaries to Washington to advise the Congress of events in Oregon. One of these ambassadors was Joe Meek, who had friends in the Polk administration. News of the massacre caused the U.S. Congress to pass a bill in August 1848 that officially created the Territory of Oregon.

Joe Lewis was not among those punished for the attack. As soon as he saw that Waiilatpu was no longer a secure place for himself, he slipped away with two companions from the tribe. It is not possible to verify any of the stories told about him from that time on. One of the more plausible ones tells that he killed his two companions one night as they lay sleeping. Taking their horses and equipment, he fled. Later, one dark night, an expressman challenged him on a trail in what is now Idaho. Lewis failed to observe the challenge. The guard fired and killed the man who had caused so much trouble for the Oregon Country.[212]

When the last Oregon Volunteer left the mission in the late summer of 1848, Waiilatpu lay deserted and desolate. Occasionally, a curious horseman would enter this valley of tears, stand beside the Great Grave for a moment of reflection, then ride on. Later, settlers would arrive, but now, swiftly, the adobe walls weathered into dust. Waiilatpu and Whitman's dreams lay broken and forgotten — except that a bit of Marcus' and Narcissa's spirit seemed to live on in each of the four Sagers.

A New Life

Catherine

At thirteen, serious pious Catherine would be of great value to any woman who had a family to raise. She was mature far beyond her years and had long been responsible for her younger sisters, both under Narcissa Whitman's direction and later on her own. By April, Henry Spalding was able to write: "they seem satisfied and happy. Catherine is in the family of the Rev. Mr. [William M.] Roberts, Superintendent of the Methodist mission."[213] But Catherine's arrangement was not quite that simply nor pleasantly made. Elizabeth, in her candor, supplied the details of how the Reverend Roberts got Catherine: "Mrs. J. Quinn Thornton said she would take care of my baby sister Henrietta if she could have my older sister Katie. Mrs. William Roberts, whose husband was a minister, had other ideas; she wanted Catherine, but she would not accept the care of Henrietta. Mrs. Roberts was a severe woman and she liked to have her way. She finally consented to take Henrietta too, but after taking her she gave her away, keeping only Catherine." Elizabeth described the maneuvering, "She made Mrs. Thornton give up by saying that she was sure her husband would be angry with her if she took the children."[214]

Despite this unpromising start, the next few years were good ones for Catherine. It was her belief that the Roberts "did well by me." During this time one of the Roberts boys wrote to his grandparents back in New Jersey. He mentioned that his parents had taken in an orphan by the name of Catherine Sager. This letter was printed eventually in the *Christian Advocate and Journal,* a publication of the Methodist Episcopal Church.[215] There it caught the eye of Frederick Sager who remembered that his brother, Henry, had had a daughter named Catherine when he had left for Oregon in 1844. He wrote Catherine, addressing the letter, "Somewhere in Oregon." It reached her through the post office in Salem, near which she was then living.

Earliest known photo of Catherine Sager Pringle, oldest of the girls, left; and of Henrietta Naomi Sager Sterling, youngest. (Courtesy Mrs. L. W. Armin and Mrs. Celista Platz.)

She and Elizabeth both remarked how strange they found it to write to a relative about whom they knew so little. From the tones of their letters however, one may sense the yearning the girls felt to be in contact with someone who was related to them by blood.[216]

On October 25, 1851, 16-year-old Catherine married Clark Spencer Pringle with whom she settled down to a long, satisfied married life.[217] Perhaps she remembered the day at Waiilatpu when Elizabeth had discovered a real live Methodist, and all the children had run out to see if he had horns. Anyway, she married one. Moreover, Clark Pringle went on to become a Methodist circuit rider. He and Catherine established their home on a section of farmland four miles from Salem.

Soon after she was married, Catherine sent for two of her sisters, Elizabeth and Henrietta. For the next few years these

[130]

Sagers were together again. Matilda lived only 40 miles away, but travel was so difficult in the Oregon Country that Matilda saw her sisters rarely.

Clark's and Catherine's marriage was a productive one, resulting in eight children. Catherine later referred to these years as a "sober married life." Around her, the old Oregon Country was changing rapidly. Washington and Idaho became states. Cities dotted the one-time wilderness—places like Walla Walla, Spokane, Lewiston, and Seattle. Railroads soon covered the miles that had been rough trails when she was a girl. As the early history slowly receded and life went on, Catherine found that her memories of her childhood — the Oregon Trail, the Whitmans, the massacre — were of interest to the pioneers and to the younger generation. She began to give talks about those early days in communities throughout the Pacific Northwest.

In 1881, Catherine visited the thriving town of Walla Walla, Washington, to lecture on the massacre. While there she traveled the seven miles to Waiilatpu to visit the graves of the victims. She learned from the owner of the property that William H. Gray, Whitman's one-time associate, was planning to move the remains from the Great Grave to the top of the nearby hill and to erect a suitable monument to the massacre.

As soon as she returned home, Catherine wrote to Gray: "Mr. Sweagle informed me that you were intending to remove the remains of the Victims, and bury them on top of the Hill. My sisters and myself will enter a protest to this." She continued, "We certainly have some interest in the matter as our Brothers are among them. And we think it useless to disturb them after so many years have passed away." Should her arguments not make any impression on Gray, Catherine did not hesitate to add: "I wish to be present at the laying of the Monument or what ever ceremony you have at the time."[218]

After learning that Catherine Pringle was a sister of the Sager boys, Gray tried to persuade her that the remains could be better protected if they were moved to the hill. He noted that there was always the danger of the present site being converted to agricultural purposes, then the graves would be lost forever. In her reply Catherine wrote that already the markers for the

Above is earliest known photo of Great Grave, Waiilatpu. The mound of earth was put over it by Myron Eells in the 1860s. The Eells home in the background was built on the mission site. Below is the present stone on the Great Grave. John and Francis Sager are ninth and tenth of the names of the 14 who lost their lives because of the Cayuses' attack, 1847. (Courtesy Whitman Mission NHS.)

graves of Louise Sager and Helen Mar Meek had disappeared and that their graves could no longer be located. Still, she felt it would be wrong to move the remains. As for the area being plowed, she was certain that public sentiment would forbid such a deed no matter what the intentions of the property's owner might be. In any case, she announced she was willing to help raise funds for a monument.[219] Starting in her home area of Prineville, Oregon, she gave two lectures at which she received $13.75 from thirty people. "I will send the fund collected to the Bank at Walla Walla," she told Gray.[220]

It was not exactly a complaint, but Catherine explained to Gray that she could expect no help from her husband: "Mr. Pringle does not believe in Monuments or tombstones — or even coffins for the dead. Says he can not work for the Monument fund — that the Dr's Monument is in the heart of the people." But she did complain when she learned that the people of Walla Walla wanted to have the monument in the city rather than at the mission site. "I think," she wrote, "that if the people of W. W. want a monument in thier [*sic*] city they have been very slow about it." She concluded that the thing to do would be to let them build their monument to Whitman, "and we will go ahead and build one where he is buried."[221]

At this same time Catherine was developing her own concept of a suitable memorial to the dead. "The more I think of it the more anxious I am to get possession of the Mission site and build a home to be called the Narcissa House. I see so many poor children who are deprived of the care of their mothers.... If we could buy the place we could reproduce the buildings on a modern scale still preserving the out lines." She added: "You may think that my scheme is a wild one. It may be but still I think with united effort it could be done."[222]

But the raising of funds proved to be a slow affair and the eighties slipped away without anyone's idea coming to life. In 1884, Catherine was momentarily detracted when she read H. H. Bancroft's new *History of the Northwest Coast:* "A more untruthful volume I have never read — its sole object seems to be to malign Americans and missionaries and laud catholics and H. B. Co. Mrs. [Frances Fuller] Victor is evidently the Author and vents her spleen against Mr. Gray."[223] Long under the influence of Henry Spalding's pathological fear of the Catholic Church, Catherine was incensed by Mrs. Victor's history that contradicted the biased account of the Oregon Country, *A History of Oregon,* published by William Gray in 1870. She took refuge in her belief that Gray's history was worth two of Bancroft's any day.

In 1888, the fiftieth anniversary of the Presbyterian Synod of the Columbia was observed at Walla Walla.[224] Apparently none of the Sager sisters attended. Catherine learned later that at the observation there was a renewal of the idea of removing the remains from Waiilatpu to Whitman College. She heard that both Cushing Eells, a founder of the College, and Perrin Whitman favored the removal.[225]

By now, however, William Gray was committed to Catherine's views. He appeared at a public meeting in Walla Walla and argued that the best location for a memorial was the mission site, where the Oregon Pioneer and Historical Society had already taken steps to preserve the memory of those killed. Still, there were people of power and wealth in Walla Walla who thought the remains "of Dr. Whitman should be removed from the lonely spot of their interment and brought to this city. . . ."[226] Then, in 1889, before definite action was taken by anyone, William H. Gray died. The idea of a memorial slumbered.

As the fiftieth anniversary of the massacre — 1897 — approached, renewed interest in a fitting observation and a permanent memorial to the massacre victims sprang up throughout the Pacific Northwest. A two-day ceremony, November 29 and 30, was planned and arrangements were made to erect a granite monument on top of the hill overlooking the graves. The committee also planned to disinter temporarily the remains from the mass grave in order to build a marble vault for the massacred. Mrs. C. J. Picard, a Walla Walla "undertaker and funeral director," presented a fine metallic coffin for the remains.

When the great grave was excavated, the thing that Catherine had secretly dreaded came true. The remains were disappointingly few — five skulls and a few miscellaneous bones. The earlier excavations by the wolves had been thorough. An elaborate report by two local doctors, who decided that two of

Early observation of anniversary of Whitman massacre. Costumes indicate a pleasant day. Participants are gathered around the Great Grave that contains the remains of John and Francis Sager. Date and occasion unknown. (Courtesy Whitman Mission NHS.)

the skulls could be identified as belonging to the Whitmans, was printed in the newspapers.[227]

When Catherine read the doctors' report she was quite upset. In a long letter to the Spokane *Spokesman-Review,* October 25, she described the funeral in 1847. She wrote: "The grave was only about three feet deep. So it was soon dug into by wolves, and Mrs. Whitman's leg was dragged out and the flesh eaten off to the knee. We reburied it. Before we left the remains were again dug up, and morning after morning we would see the wolves at their ghoulish work and hear their snarling." Sadly she added: "But where the bones of Dr. Whitman and many of his associates are, God only knows. I am sorry that the grave was ever disturbed, for doubt has now become a certainty."[228]

Plans for the ceremony proceeded, and soon Catherine found herself entering the spirit of the event despite her forebodings. Although her dream of a children's home would not materialize, she ceased her opposition to what was being done. At least, the remains would stay at Waiilatpu.

At the last minute it was discovered that the marble slab for the great grave would not arrive on time. Nonetheless, the observation began Monday, November 29, in the Walla Walla opera house. It was a scene of great oratory and singing. Nine survivors of the massacre, including Catherine, Elizabeth, and Matilda, were present. The Bible was read from by the Reverend Samuel Greene, son of the Secretary of the American Board who had sent the Whitmans and the Spaldings to Oregon in 1836. Before the speeches were finished, some of the orators rekindled the flame of the smouldering belief held by no few Oregon Protestants, and long argued by Spalding and Gray, that the Roman Catholic priests and the Hudson's Bay Company were somehow responsible for the massacre. Catherine believed in this theory with all her heart. Like Spalding, she would never waver in her conviction that Brouillet and Blanchet were among the plotters of the massacre. And being an outspoken woman she expressed her beliefs about the matter throughout her life.

On the day following the anniversary, many of the participants went to the mission site aboard special trains. Despite the bad weather, a few essential addresses were made. Although

Catherine Sager Pringle, Elizabeth Sager Helm, and Matilda Sager Delaney, 1897, at the time of the 50th anniversary of the Whitman massacre. (Courtesy Mrs Celista Platz.)

none of this elaborate program had met with her original approval, Catherine had long since agreed to be a participant. She made "a brief and touching address ... which moved many to tears." Vivid memories must have passed through her mind as she stood before the Great Grave and said, "We desire to thank the people of Walla Walla and the Northwest for their presence here, for their kindness in burying our dead, and for their royal entertainment." How well she estimated the future: "These acts of kindness will be told to our children's children and be carried down to the future generations in grateful remembrance as each recurring anniversary passes."[229]

The large marble slab that still covers the vault arrived in January 1898, and on the 29th of that month, "a burial service was conducted by ... [the] pastors of the Congregational and Presbyterian churches of Walla Walla; the coffin was placed in the vault, and the massive slab of marble, weighing two tons, was lowered in its place and sealed."[230] Inscribed on it are fourteen names, the ninth and tenth being John and Francis Sager.

On August 10, 1910, at the home of her youngest daughter, Lucia Pringle Collins, at Spokane, Washington, near the site of the Tshimakain mission station that she had visited as a girl in 1847, Catherine Sager Pringle, aged 75, died. Her granddaughter, Sadie Collins Armin, recalls Catherine's last years in Spokane: "She was the most comforting, most kind, calm and tranquil person I ever knew. Yet she had a most keen sense of humor and her eyes would light up and sparkle and her face beam with a mischievous smile." Mrs. Armin remembers, too, that "physically she was a small person, stood about five feet tall, was slightly stooped and of course her hard and busy life had etched wrinkles on her face. She really was fragile looking, like a china tea-cup or a dresden doll, but oh, so capable."

Hers had been a full rich life, and the events that she witnessed were of an era that had already passed from the American scene. Her adventure had become a part of the nation's history.

Elizabeth

Although possessing the gentle disposition and air of optimism that she shared with her sisters, Elizabeth was not to find a permanent home among the settlers' families. Many years later she recalled her arrival in the Willamette, telling an interviewer that "the thing she remembered best was the awful homesickness. She, who had no home, was heartsick for the want of one. She was separated at once from her sisters, in finding new places of shelter after the rescue."[231] During the seven years between her arrival on the Willamette and her marriage in 1855, Elizabeth lived in six different homes.

In the first year she moved from a Mrs. William Johnson to a Mrs. Howland, then to the Jacob Robb family. Settling down for two years with the Robbs, Elizabeth might have found security with them, but for the discovery of gold in California, which stripped nearly all the Oregon homes of their men. Robb first went to the mines in the fall of 1848 with William Abernethy. Mrs. Robb, her two children, and Elizabeth moved into Mrs. Abernethy's house for the winter. The summer of 1849 was spent with Mrs. Robb's father, the Reverend E. E. Parrish of Parrish's Gap, south of Salem. Parrish remembered the Sagers well. It had been he who had recorded in his diary on the prairies in 1844 that there had been a frolic in the Sager family at the time Henrietta was born. However, in 1849, he made little impression on Elizabeth. She took care of her stay at his home in one sentence in her reminiscences.

In the fall of 1850, Robb returned to Oregon for his family. Elizabeth, not wanting to go to California, was forced to find a new home. She spent the next year, 1850-51, with William H. Willson's family in Salem. During that year she paid for her keep by doing the housework. More importantly, however, she was able to spend part of her time attending the Oregon Institute, the first schooling she had had since Waiilatpu. But it did not work out; the Willsons "were so unkind to me I would not stay any longer. So I went to live with Mr. [Josiah L.] Parrish."[232] Mrs. Parrish was a new and different experience for Elizabeth. The poor woman's mental condition caused her to be quite unpredictable. At one moment she would be solicitous and extraordinarily kind to the girl, then later would berate her for the very same actions that had aroused the earlier sentiments. This arrangement did not last long, and the end came about because of Matilda.

Although Matilda lived not far away (about two days' travel), Elizabeth had seen her but once in the more than three years since they had left the mission. Catherine, now a new bride, decided she should visit Matilda and she wanted Elizabeth to go with her. Elizabeth approached Mrs. Parrish and told her about the plans for the trip. Mrs. Parrish was in one of her moods at the time and became quite irked at Elizabeth's insistence on making the trip. In the end, Elizabeth ignored the woman's threats and went with Catherine. When she returned to the Parrish home, Elizabeth was told to pack her possessions; she no longer had a home there. It was then she decided to live with Catherine and Clark.

Determined to be independent, to rely on no one for material needs, and to live in no more foster homes, Elizabeth, 16 years old and with little training, began teaching school. She taught three years. That was a long time to be an attractive young school teacher in woman-shy Oregon. Catherine thought it needed some explanation when writing Uncle Frederick:

"Elizabeth is teaching school. She has taught off and on for the last three years. I do not know if she will marry or not. She is engaged but will not marry she says till she has made something."[233]

In 1853, at a revival meeting on the Calapooia River, Elizabeth had met a young man named William Fletcher Helm, the son of an 1845 immigrant of the same name. During the next two years while she was teaching "off and on," she saw more of young William and finally agreed to marry him. The wedding took place on August 9, 1855. Apparently, Elizabeth had "made something."

Like Catherine, Elizabeth lived a long happy "sober married life." A few of William's letters to her have survived and it is apparent she picked a gentle, thoughtful, if unambitious husband, whose loneliness when he had to leave her for even a short time disclosed his need for Elizabeth. Their marriage produced no fewer than nine children, eight of whom survived both William and Elizabeth.

Like her surviving sisters, Elizabeth became interested in the plans concerning commemorating those killed at Waiilatpu in 1847. Only one of her letters concerning this matter has been located. In January 1890 she wrote Myron Eells saying that she felt "reconciled and satisfyed" in having the remains moved, adding that she had "no doubt their graves will be better cared for if removed to a place where it can be better approached." She mentioned her uncertainty about all the remains being in the grave where they had first been placed. She hoped to visit the old mission site that coming spring to inspect the Great Grave and to see if she could find Louise's grave marker. Until she made the journey she asked Eells to await her final opinion on any removal. Whether or not she made the spring trip is unknown.

In her 88th year, at Portland, Oregon, Elizabeth Sager Helm died on July 19, 1925, ten years after her husband. Before her death she told the president of Whitman College at Walla Walla, Dr. S. B. L. Penrose, about her experience at Waiilatpu. She summed up her three years at the mission, saying: "I have now the Bible of my own that Mr. Rodgers had written my name in, and my daughter Mary has a Testament that belonged

National Park Service visitor center at Whitman Mission. Its museum tells the story of the Sagers and other children at Waiilatpu. (Courtesy Whitman Mission NHS.)

to my brother John when he left Ohio. This is all that remains to me of that part of my life."[234] That, and the memories.

Henrietta

The history of Henrietta Naomi Sager's later years is a brief one. Because of her very young age and few memories of the mission and the massacre, one sees her always through the eyes of others — whether it be the Reverend Parrish recording her birth, or Narcissa Whitman describing how she coaxed the baby from the edge of the grave to health, or Catherine telling how she comforted her baby sister through that long first night of the massacre. There is no known letter or diary written by Henrietta herself.

When the survivors came down from Waiilatpu, Henrietta was a problem. No woman, except Mrs. Thornton, wanted to take on the burden of raising a three-year-old child. Mrs. Roberts took her only to give her away at the first opportunity. The name of this foster-parent has escaped history. Catherine wrote simply: "My sister was soon after taken by a lady who had no children."[235] The only mention found of Henrietta during these first years in the lower country is in the 1850 census. There she is listed as being in the Morgan Kees household, Linn County.[236] When Catherine married in 1851, Henrietta came to live with her. She was then seven years old, ready to feel a sense of permanency for places and things.

The discovery of gold in California affected all Americans in the 1850's, Henrietta as much as anyone. It first crossed her path when one of her uncles, Solomon Sager, arrived in California in 1856. Possibly on the way to El Dorado, but more likely making a trip to Oregon after arriving in California, Solomon visited Catherine and Clark in Salem. Henrietta listened to her uncle tell the Pringles of his plans. He had come west for his wife's health. (She was to die later of tuberculosis.) California was his choice and he already had a plan for supporting his family. He could not rely upon the risky business of searching for gold; his wealth would come from entertaining the miners with the Sager Dramatic Troupe.

Had she produced lightning, Henrietta would not have shocked her sister and brother-in-law more than she did by announcing her intention of accompanying Uncle Solomon as a member of the troupe of entertainers. To Catherine, formed in the same moral mold as Narcissa Whitman, the thought of her sister becoming an actress left her almost breathless. Clark, as straight-laced as his wife, felt the same. Although Solomon's troupe would hardly seem to be a wicked group of loose-living actors, as actors were imagined to be then as in later times, the Pringles were not certain of the propriety of the idea. They considered the California gold mines to be no place for an orphan girl.[237]

When Henrietta left for California as a member of Uncle Solomon's troupe, her sisters felt that she had almost, if not in fact, disgraced the family. Even though the Sager Dramatic Troupe was composed of mostly cousins, including Della Sager who would later gain fame on her own as an actress, there would be temptations facing a young girl in the mining camps. The reviews of the troupe were favorable; the audiences in San Francisco, Sacramento, and the northern mines liked the traveling Sagers. In 1858 Henrietta even had the chance of seeing her sister, Matilda Hazlitt, when the troupe played Henley, California, then Matilda's home town.

The record is not clear, but it may have been this occasion when the other sisters learned that Henrietta had succumbed to those aspects of an actress' life that they considered risque, if not immoral. Whatever the exact circumstances were, Henrietta soon cleared her reputation by returning to Oregon and marrying Jno. L. Cooper, on October 23, 1860.[238]

Very little is known of her experiences following this marriage. There was a flurry of correspondence between her and her sisters for a short time — as if indicating that she was back in their good graces. In 1861 Matilda received a letter from her and, a year later, Matilda wrote to Elizabeth: "An acquaintance of mine came from the Northern mines not long ago. He said that he got acquainted with her [Henrietta's] husband. He says that he is a very nice steady young man."[239] At this same time Catherine wrote to Henry Spalding, "Henrietta was in San Francisco when I heard from her last. Her husband was sick. She does not write to me any more. I do not know why she does not."[240]

[143]

Catherine must have known why Henrietta preferred not writing. Her experiences were far different from the others; her life was not that of her sisters, who had been old enough to be greatly influenced by Narcissa's Whitman's precepts.

The next mention of Henrietta by the family was negative in tone. Matilda wrote her sisters in July 1863: "Adella [Della Sager] did not know anything about H. She inquired very particularly about her."[241] Henrietta supplied the answer of her whereabouts in the last known letter she wrote, in 1864. She informed Matilda that she was then living in Marysville, California.[242] But her stay there must have been short. In the fall of 1865, Matilda wrote that "the letter that I wrote her came back through the dead letter office." As far as it may be determined, none of the sisters heard directly from Henrietta again.

In the Whitman College Library today is a letter that, from appearances, Henry Spalding wrote to Henrietta in the fall of 1866. Strikingly strange is a penned note found at the end of the letter: "Found in the street in San Francisco." Did Henrietta drop it? What was its subsequent history? An analysis of its content indicates that only Henry Spalding could have been its author. It is dated Brownsville, Oregon, October 25, 1866.

Spalding began: "You may think I have forgotten you & the kindness you manifested to me at Lewiston by not writing before." What was Henrietta doing in Lewiston, then a gold mining town? He informed her that a Brother Condon at The Dalles had taken "your names [?] to see if any letters in Express Office, said he would write to you. Was glad to hear from you, is your friend." Spalding reported that he had "not yet seen Catherine or Elizabeth," adding that he hoped to visit them that fall. He hoped that Henrietta's health was improved and he thanked her for the gift of a cane. Toward the end, his comments imply that Henrietta was not just a visitor to Lewiston but perhaps lived there: "Write & let me know all about Lewiston, and about the mines on Paluse & at Warren's Diggings. Does Belcher remain merchant at Lewiston." He concluded by asking her to give his best regards to her husband.[243]

In 1868 Catherine wrote Spalding saying, "We never hear from Henrietta. If you do please let us know."[244] Perhaps this plea indicated that Catherine and her sisters were ready to reconcile with Henrietta. If so, they were too late. Two years later, her sisters learned that Henrietta was dead. It is said that at Red Bluff, California, an unknown assailant, intending to shoot her husband, shot and killed her.[245]

The mystery of this event is deepened by two letters to Elizabeth from a first cousin in Ohio named Maggie Sager Dockum. In her first letter, dated December 4, 1877, Maggie wrote: "I had not heard of Henrietta's death. I have her picture, her husband Mr. Sterling sent hers and his picture to us some six or seven years ago. We exchanged several letters, and then through neglect our correspondence ceased. Did she leave any children?" Besides introducing the name of Sterling, of whom nothing else is known, Maggie further compounded the mystery when she wrote again in March 1878: "The last letter we had from him [Sterling] he was in New York City, said he had been expecting his wife but the steamer he had expected to bring her had arrived and she had not come, and he should return to California, and we never heard from them since until you told us of her death."[246]

Who was Sterling? Was he Henrietta's second husband? Had Cooper died or divorced her, and had she married again? The record is not clear. Perhaps history will eventually shed more light on her short, troubled life.

From the glimpses that may be seen, her brief, shadowy history reflected the substance of her life. Orphaned when only a few months old, torn from her new parents when only three, passed around as an unwanted burden until Catherine was married, she had no roots in the Presbyterian sense of propriety that imbued her sisters with their sense of destiny. Although a career on the stage shocked her sisters, it possibly gave Henrietta the only sense of achievement she had ever known. History records that she married at least once, but it does not now disclose what other tumultous affairs of the heart she may have experienced.

In her short life of 26 years, she witnessed the history of the West — the Oregon Trail, the mission era, massacre, captivity, pioneer settlement, the gold rush, and the frontier theater. One would be in error to assume that her life was less than vital in the settlement of the Far West.

Matilda

Matilda had celebrated her eighth birthday a month before the massacre. Into those few years had been packed a lifetime of adventure and tragedy. In retrospect, they must have remained an important time in her memory; but the rest of her life was also vividly marked with high adventure and further tragedy. The remarkable thing about this person, when endless sorrow should have seared her soul, was her unending faith in human beings and an unfailing sense of humor. Her dry wit failed to conceal a perpetual kindness for the unfortunate. Hers was not a easy outpouring of love however; it was sterner stuff. Still, her love of humanity was deep and it was real.

On arriving in the Willamette she first stayed with the Spaldings. During the four months she lived with them, she attended Mrs. Thornton's private school that was held in the nearby Methodist church. In the spring of 1848, Spalding moved to Forest Grove, staying with Alvin T. Smith until a new house was built. Matilda moved with him.

No one bothered to consult with her when it was decided she should move to the home of a man named William Geiger, Jr., who had a farm not far away. The first time Geiger came after Matilda, she cried so hard that it was decided she should not move just then. A day or two later he came again, and again Matilda refused to leave with him, clinging in panic to the Spaldings' hired girl, Mary Johnson. But by the time Geiger made his third trip, Matilda's resistance had broken down. She packed her few belongings and climbed up on the horse behind the stranger.[247]

Geiger, who had known Narcissa Whitman in New York, had come to Oregon in 1839. He had arrived as a settler, but one interested in American Board mission activities. Following adventures in Hawaii and California, he had assumed the caretaking of the Whitman mission during the winter of 1842-43 when the doctor was on his trip to the East. Settling finally in the Willamette Valley, he practiced medicine (and was called doctor), served in such public offices as county clerk and surveyor, and farmed. Still a new bridegroom when Matilda came to live with him, Geiger ruled his household fiercely. Religion and sin were never far from his mind and with strict and severe discipline, he carried out his duties as he saw them as guardian of Matilda and her morals.[248]

Matilda learned early that Geiger was a man who believed in direct action. This trait was illustrated the night that poor Mrs. Geiger developed a terrible toothache. The pain was so severe that she got up to walk the floor. His sleep ruined, Geiger got up too. He found a steel punch and a hammer. Mrs. Geiger lost the offending tooth and at last sleep settled over the household.[249]

If it took Matilda a while to adjust to the Geigers, she found some of the neighbors even stranger. She remembered the farmer who did not believe in working on Sunday to the extent that he refused to feed his cow — although he would milk her. The hungry cow would bawl for her feed, then on Monday the farmer would punish her by whipping the dumb beast for her Sunday bawling.[250]

Matilda had scarcely settled in with the Geigers in their one-room log cabin, when her guardian caught the gold fever. Sending his wife and Matilda to live with his father-in-law, the Reverend J. A. Cornwall, Geiger left for California. The winter in the Cornwall home was pleasant enough, although the old man's incompetence in managing his farm threw much of the heavy work on the women, including Matilda. Since Geiger had no money to leave for them to live on, his wife spent the winter knitting socks for other would-be miners, selling them at one dollar a pair. Matilda recalled her winter duties with a shudder: "It was my job to pull the wool off the dead sheep [that froze to death from lack of attention] and wash it in the creek. . . . Washing the dirt and grease out of the wool in the ice cold water, was a heart-breaking job." But Mrs. Geiger had to have the wool for her knitting or they would all go hungry.

The valley was still a primitive land in the winter of 1848-49, and Matilda faced a dilemma that she never did resolve. When sent on an errand to a neighboring farm, she could not decide whether it was safer to stay in the open country to get chased and treed by the wild long-horned cattle that roamed the unfenced land, or to go through the timber to avoid the cattle and to take her chances with a hungry wolf pack.

Geiger returned from California in 1849 and again settled

in the small cabin. Catherine Pringle summed up the next six years of Matilda's life with the Geigers by saying she "is like a daughter to them." But there were problems. At first, Geiger refused to let Matilda attend school, Sunday school, or church. He was feuding with all three institutions because of doctrinal differences in Biblical interpretations. A break for the better came into Matilda's life in the spring of 1850 and again in 1851, when Cushing Eells, Whitman's former co-worker, opened a school at Forest Grove. It cost Geiger $5 for each of the two 3-month terms to send Matilda, but he allowed her to attend. Two years later, Eells opened a new school in Hillsboro and again Matilda was allowed to attend by working for her board. That was all the formal education she was to get. She spent her last two years of single life back on the Geiger farm.[251]

Life with the Geigers was not all serious work, not when one was a Sager. From time to time laughter broke into the simple strict discipline of Matilda's life. One such time was when Matilda saw a town pump for the first time. "I had read of town pumps, but had never seen one until I went there [to Hillsboro] and I did not like the taste of the water in this, but Mr. Griffin[252] said it was sulfur water. Finally it got so strong of sulfur he concluded he had better have the well cleaned out. . . . They found a side of bacon, a skunk, some squirrels and mice."[253]

On July 4, 1850, William Geiger became the legal guardian of Matilda "from and immediately after the date of the appointment, until the aforesaid Minor shall attain to the age of eighteen."[254] He carried out his obligations of guardian seriously. Five years later, when attempting to obtain for Matilda a quarter section of land to which she seemed to be entitled, he offered to resign his guardianship in favor of Clark Pringle, who was doing the same for Henrietta and Elizabeth. However, the matter was put before Matilda and she decided that she preferred to have Geiger continue as her guardian.[255]

By 1855 fifteen-year-old Matilda was in love. In January she had become engaged to a young man named Lewis Mackey Hazlitt. Lewis and his partner, who was Geiger's brother, were operating a store for miners in Cottonwood, northern California. After the engagement Lewis returned to California, promising to come back to make Matilda his bride. By May he had not yet

Matilda Sager and her first husband, Lewis M. Hazlitt.
(Courtesy Whitman College.)

returned and Matilda felt she had been jilted. Broken-hearted, she wrote her sisters imploring them never to mention his name again. This is the earliest known letter between the Sager girls:

May 20, 1855

Dearly Loved Sisters:

It is with pleasure that I now write to you. We are all well at present. I received your letters and defered answering them until I found out how things were going to turn. I am not married yet and do not know if there is any prospect of it. Mr. hasn't been true to his promise and if he does come I don't know if I will have him. I hope you will forgive and forget anything that I have written that has hurt your feelings and love your distant sister as well as you ever did. We have been raised so far apart that it hardly seems like I have sisters but we will all be old friends again like we used to.

I have one favor to ask of you, that is that you will never mention Lewis name to me again as I want to forget it, that is in answer, for it makes me sad to hear his name. Will you burn all the letters that I have wrote you so that the sight of them won't mar the pleasure that you see all together, and once in awhile indulge me by thinking of me.

Mr. Geiger is going to build this summer. I am going to stay home during the summer and go to school in the fall and winter. Mr. G. will write a few lines to Clark about the land. I can't come to see you this summer but would like to.

There is great excitement about settling the Cayuse country [the Whitman mission area]. Perhaps I will too if I get a chance to go. You must all write to me when you can. I wish I could see my little nephew.

[149]

I wish you had called him Francis Henry after Father. I have not heard from the States yet. If I could I would kiss you all but I can't and content myself with sending one. Please excuse my writing as I feel a little excited you know. Give my love to all my friends and believe me ever

Your affecionate sister
M. J. Sager

The book mark give to Henrietta and when I make some more I will send the rest some.

The ribbon will do to piece something for the baby.[256]

But the letter was soon out of date. Lewis finally showed up and Matilda promptly forgot that her heart had been broken. There would be no school for her that fall and no pioneering in the Cayuse country.

The wedding was held on June 5.[257] It was an elegant affair for Oregon and a number of Matilda's old mission friends were present. Abigail Walker, whom Stanley had painted at Tshimakain, helped her to dress. Abigail's father, Elkanah Walker, performed the ceremony. Mrs. Cushing Eells came to watch. And the wedding cake was baked by Mary Walker. All told, it was a very fine affair, and very proper. The bride was given a grand send-off to her new home in California.

Although there was trouble occasionally between the Indians and the settlers in northern California, the Hazlitts prospered, not in gold mining nor in store keeping, but in cattle and farming. They made their home in Henley, later called Cottonwood, a trading center for the mines. Their good times lasted only five years. In 1860, Lewis developed cancer and he and Matilda traveled to San Francisco where he was operated on. Two years later, Matilda wrote that the cancer had reappeared. "He is going to try and go to the City again to be operated on again this winter," she informed her sisters. "It cost a great deal to go but we have no confidence in any of the surgeons around here." She added: "We think of selling off everything and buying a good sewing machine and trying to make a living at that."[258]

The winter of 1862-63 was a terribly severe time, much like the bitter winter of 1846-47 at Waiilatpu. When the storms had passed, almost all of Hazlitt's herd of 500 cattle had died. With spring, Lewis made the lonely frightful journey to San Francisco without his wife. On June 18, Matilda wrote, "My darling is gone." She described the tragedy: "He died in San Francisco the 14th inst. away from home among strangers with no kind hand of affection to smooth his last hours of life. Oh, if [I] could just have seen him before he died."[259]

A widow at 24, with five children to care for, Matilda could afford the luxury of loneliness and sorrow only in those few minutes of privacy she reserved for herself. She wrote her sisters that with reasonable effort she would be able to make ends meet. Lewis had left her a lot on which she planned to build a house. There were 75 head of cattle that would provide beef, butter, and milk. The garden would produce a surplus that would bring in a few dollars; and there was a fine orchard that her husband had so carefully nurtured. At the end of her first year as a widow, she wrote of her continuing loneliness, "I have worked harder this summer than I ever have since I was married. I have got along very well so far. I take in some washing and sell some beef cattle and [with] what the garden brings me I get along very comfortably."[260]

The new house was ready for occupancy that September. This home was very important to Matilda, as was shown in her letter to Elizabeth: "It is not near finished but it is comfortable. It seems so much better than living in other people's houses. I have been so long without a home of my own that I know how to appreciate it. I have been busy the last week in setting out my rose bushes and flowers and shade trees around it. I want it to look nice." She added, "Send me some pretty flower seeds if you can get any for I want to have the prettiest place around here."[261] Narcissa Whitman's lessons in botany and beauty were still influencing her children.

The gold mines were playing out by the early 1860's, and Henley's prosperity declined with them. Miners and tradesmen left for newer digs and poverty settled over the partially-deserted community. This depression, marked by an increase in prices because of the Civil War, made Matilda a determined Democrat. In November, 1864, she expressed her opinion of President Lincoln: "Provisions are very high, flour is seven cents a pound, groceries coming up all the time. I think if this war lasts much longer we had all as well quit living, for the taxes a person has to pay would break a rich man, let alone a poor one. You say that you are all Republicans and hope I am one. You are very much mistaken for I am a Democrat to the backbone and think that every man who voted for old Abe will pray God to forgive him before another four years rolls 'round. I think that free America is about gone in."

Several times during the years following Lewis' death, Matilda mentioned the name of another of her husband's partners, Matthew Fultz. "Mat," as she called him, was a source of strength in helping Matilda to take care of the cattle, orchards, and children. She wrote of him: "He is so kind and good to me and the children. If it was not for him I don't know how I would get along. He is truly a friend indeed."[262]

In the autumn of 1865, two years a widow, Matilda agreed to marry Matthew: "Sister, I am going to get married again, to Mat Fultz. It is no use for me to try to live singly and try to raise a family."[263] A year later, a baby girl, the first of three, was born to Matilda and Mat. "We call her Ida Leona. Mat is very proud of her. She is a pretty child. The other children are all fond of her."[264]

In 1868 Matilda took her family north to visit her sisters and the Geiger family in Oregon. It was a good trip and the families were kept busy becoming acquainted with one another. On the way back to California, Matilda took time to visit old Dr. Dagon, her champion of those days so long ago on the Oregon Trail. "He looked very pale and bad, he said he had been quite unwell."[265] It did not seem possible that 24 years had passed since the long journey west.

The passage of time came with a jolt in 1875 when Matilda's first-born left home. The wrench in her heart showed in a letter to Elizabeth: "Henry left home the 20th of Dec., he is carrying the mail on the Lake City and Big Valley route. If any of you want to write him direct to Dorris Bridge, Modoc Co., Cal. Well, I think it is best for him to go for himself. Mat never done just right with him. Hays has got to be a big boy, and he is a good boy. So is Henry, if he lives he will make just such a man as his father."[266]

In 1882 Matthew and Matilda sold their home at Henley and moved to Farmington, Washington. There they invested their savings in a hotel. Other side businesses grew up quickly.

However, within a year Matthew died, leaving Matilda a widow for the second time. She now found herself running a hotel, a furniture store, a livery stable, and an undertaking business. Such a capable businesswoman was bound to catch the eye of David Delaney, Farmingham's most prosperous citizen and largest landowner.[267] In 1889 Matilda accepted his challenge and found herself a bride for the third time.[268]

One year before her third marriage, when she learned of the plans the Walla Walla citizens had for moving the massacre victims to Whitman College, Matilda joined Catherine in opposition. In September 1888, she wrote a letter to the *Walla Walla Journal* saying that she had learned, mistakenly, that the remains had already been moved. She blamed Perrin Whitman for "this act of vandalism." Her protest was centered on the fact that the ashes of her brothers were "comingled with those of Dr. Whitman and wife," thus how could Perrin authorize their removal without the Sagers' permission. Reacting emotionally, she wrote: "Perrin Whitman knew that I and my sisters were decidedly opposed to any disturbance of our sacred dead, and he should have had at least manhood enough to withhold his consent until he could notify us."

Matilda's attack on Perrin was not fully justified. The real planners behind the proposed move were the monied families of Walla Walla, who also gave generous support to Whitman College. Their intentions were honorable; however they obviously had failed to consult the Sager sisters concerning their plans. To Matilda this was a breach of manners and faith.

The Walla Walla paper appended an editorial comment to Matilda's letter, titled "Getting Hot in the Collar." Although editorials were direct, personal, and often vindictive in that age of individualism, this one appears today to have been unusually mean. It denied any ulterior motives on the part of those who wished to remove the remains. It chided Matilda for her abusive language — language which it said it omitted from the printed letter. Then the editor added: "If on the day of removal, you desire the bones of your brothers to remain where they are, you can come and pick them out and do with them as seemeth best to you." To Matilda's credit, this bitter attack apparently did not affect her normal good spirits.

Walla Walla, 1889. The three surviving Sager sisters came here to observe the 50th anniversary of the massacre in 1897. Whitman College is represented by the small tower in the far distance to the right of center. (Courtesy Penrose Memorial Library, Whitman College.)

Matilda too attended the 1897 anniversary observations at Waiilatpu. It was she who was asked to inspect the bones of the 1847 interment. Contrary to Catherine, she pronounced herself fully satisfied with the disinterment and with the plans for the memorial — now that it was to be at the mission.

As the years increased, Matilda became seriously ill with rheumatism. At times her limbs were almost paralyzed and her doctor was ready to give her up to death. She did not die, and when he told her she would never walk again she determined to prove him wrong. "I at last recovered the use of my limbs," she wrote proudly, and "with my sister I went to visit Perrin Whitman, our old friend."[270] These three must have had much to talk about from the days when they were young together at Waiilatpu. Possibly, she had learned by then that Perrin had not been the plotter behind the idea to remove the massacre victims to Whitman College in 1888. Now there would be much that needed not the saying among the three — just the remembering.

While on this trip to Lewiston, Matilda received word that the hotel had burned to the ground and that all her possessions had been destroyed. She was no longer young and this loss was a great shock to her. Lesser people might have surrendered long before this, but now even Matilda knew defeat: "Since then I have never been able to do anything, but have been cared for by my children." She outlived her third husband and her last years were spent quietly and in as much ease as attacks of pain would allow. Still interested in her Oregon Country, she attended the reunion of the Oregon Pioneer Society at Portland in 1916. Her last days were spent in the sunny warmth of Reseda, California, at the home of her youngest daughter. Still busily working on her plans to write another book of recollections, Matilda Jane, the last of the seven Sagers, died on April 13, 1928. The trek of Henry and Naomi and their seven children had begun 84 years ago when Oregon was still largely a vision. The journey now reached an end.

Footnotes

1. Most of the data concerning the Sager family history was made available by three of the Sagers' grandchildren: Mrs. Guy Carpenter, San Francisco (granddaughter of Matilda Sager), Mrs. L. W. Armin, Sioux Falls, and Mrs. Harry Platz, Seattle (both granddaughters of Catherine Sager). Also useful were Fred Lockley, *Oregon Trail Blazers* (New York, 1929), and a typed unsigned family history, "The Sager Family," Whitman College Library, Walla Walla, Washington.
2. Catherine Sager Pringle, "My Story," ms, pp. 1-2. Two typescripts of this manuscript are known to exist. They differ slightly, mostly on matters concerning spelling and style. Nearly all the citations that follow are from the Meany copy. The few taken from the other are identified by "WMNHS." The Bibliography discusses the manuscript further.
3. Matilda Sager Delaney, *A Survivor's Recollections of the Whitman Massacre* (Spokane, 1920), 7. Matilda claimed Missouri as her birthplace. Her sister, Elizabeth, in Lockley, *Oregon Trail Blazers*, 324-25, said Matilda was born just before the family moved from Ohio. This confusion is illustrative of the continuous movement of the Sagers and their being orphaned in childhood.
4. Matilda Sager Delaney Collection, Whitman College Library. Pringle, p. 1.
5. *Ibid.*
6. Verne Bright, "The Folklore and History of the 'Oregon Fever,'" *Oregon Historical Quarterly*, LII (1951), 241. Hereafter cited as *OHQ*.
7. Ray Allen Billington, *The American Frontier*, points out that the great movements to the west happened only in times of prosperity.
8. Ray Allen Billington, *The Far Western Frontier, 1830-1860* (New York, 1956), 68, 85-90. In this study, Billington discusses the motivations of the emigrants of the 1840's.
9. Pringle, p. 1. Henry's restlessness made a lasting impression in the minds of his daughters.
10. Irene Paden, *Wake of the Prairie Schooner* (New York, 1947), 54. F. G. Young, "The Oregon Trail," *OHQ*, I (1900), 339-70.
11. Paden, 54. Young, 354.
12. For conflicting reports on Naomi Sager's state of mind, see Pringle, p. 2. "Father ... had been talking of going to Texas. But Mother, hearing much said about the healthfulness of Oregon, preferred to go there." Elizabeth Sager Helm, letter to Frederick Sager, January 17, 1855, in Myra Helm, *Lorinda Bewley and the Whitman Massacre* (Portland, 1951), 82-87. Clifford M. Drury, *Marcus Whitman, M.D., Pioneer and Martyr* (Caldwell, 1937), 234.
13. In general, oxen were preferred over mules. While oxen were slow — 12 to 15 miles a day — they were steady and could thrive on anything green or brown. If an ox went lame, it could be butchered and added to the larder. Also, Indians were less interested in oxen than in horses and mules. Finally, their price was in their favor — 3 oxen could be purchased for the price of one mule. Paden, 16. George R. Stewart, *The California Trail* (New York, 1962), 40, 114-15.
14. *Ibid.*, Chapter 4. David Lavender, *Westward Vision, The Story of the Oregon Trail* (New York, 1963), 387. Dale Morgan, editor, *Overland In 1846, Diaries and Letters of the California-Oregon Trail*, I, 17-18, and 18n.

15. Lavender, 388. H. S. Lyman, "Reminiscences of Wm. M. Case," *OHQ*, I (1900), 272.
16. W. J. Ghent, *The Road to Oregon, A Chronicle of the Great Emigrant Trail* (New York, 1929), 81-84.
17. *Ibid.* Ghent notes that the figures given by many for the number to leave the Missouri amount to over 1,000, while the number arriving on the Pacific Coast is less than 900, probably not more than 600-700. There were relatively few deaths on the trail that year. The discrepancy is still to be resolved. Another discussion on the number of immigrants arriving is in Lavender, 388. A "Roll of Oregon Pioneers Who Came to Oregon in 1844' was prepared by the Oregon Pioneer Association. It lists 210 males, presumably adults, and one woman, also there was someone named "Big Sis." Copy of the Roll is at the Oregon Historical Society, Portland. Hereafter referred to as OHS. The census quoted in the text is from a letter by Cornelius Gilliam in the *Daily Missouri Republican*, May 28, 1844, reprinted in Nebraska State Historical Society, *Publications*, XX, 126.
18. Pringle, p. 2.
19. John Minto, "Antecedents of the Oregon Pioneers and the Light These Throw on Their Motives," *OHQ*, V (1904), 53.
20. Hubert H. Bancroft, *History of Oregon* (San Francisco, 1886), I, 488.
21. *Ibid.;* Fred Lockley, "Reminiscences of Mrs. Frank Collins, nee Martha Elizabeth Gilliam," *OHQ*, XVII (1916), 360.
22. Bancroft, I, 448.
23. E. E. Parrish, "E. E. Parrish's Traveling Diary Across the plains," MS, entry for May 16, 1844, Idaho Historical Society, Boise, Idaho. See also Bancroft, I, 448n.
24. John Minto, "Reminiscences of Honorable John Minto, Pioneer of 1844," *OHQ*, II (1901), 133; Bancroft, I, 448, lists the 4 captains as R. W. Morrison, William Shaw, Richard Woodcock, and Elijah Bunton. John Minto, "Robert Wilson Morrison," *Transactions of the ... Oregon Pioneers Association, 1894* (Hereafter cited as *TOPA*), 56, names A. Saunders in place of Bunton. Besides a captain, each company had a lieutenant, first and second sergeants, an orderly sergeant, and first and second corporals. See Harrison C. Dale, "The Organization of the Oregon Emigrating Companies," *OHQ*, XVI (1915), 220. The Woodcock company left the train early on the trip and the others did not see it again until eastern Oregon country. Minto, "Reminiscenses," *OHQ*, II (1901), 223.
25. Minto, *ibid.*, 141; T. C. Shaw, "Capt. William Shaw," *TOPA*, 1887, 49-50.
26. Mrs. Morrison states the wives' point of view toward the overland journey better than any of her companions. When asked why she had worked so hard in getting ready for the trip that she did not relish, she replied simply, "Wilson wished to go."
27. Minto, "Antecedents," *OHQ*, V (1904), 40. Minto is not convincing when he argues that these emigrants were predestined to "save Oregon" from the British. A brief biographical sketch of Minto is found in Bancroft, I, 451n.
28. Minto, "Reminiscences," *OHQ*, II (1901), 123; Theresa Gay, *James W. Marshall, The Discoverer of California Gold, A Biography* (Georgetown, The Talisman Press, 1967), 45-46.
29. S. D. Flora, "The Great Flood of 1844 Along the Kansas and Marais des Cygnes Rivers," *The Kansas Historical Quarterly*, XX (1952), 73-81.
30. Pringle, p. 3.
31. *Ibid.*
32. Parrish; Vernon Carstensen, "Diary of Samuel Black Crockett, 1844," in Washington State Historical Society, *Building a State, Washington, 1889-1939* (Tacoma, 1940), 600. In later years Henrietta celebrated her birthday on May 22.
33. The "bound over for good behavior" sentence is recorded in Parrish, entry for June 5. The staking-out sentence was told by W. H. Rees in Bancroft, I, 450n.

34. Minto, "Reminiscences," *OHQ,* II (1901), 141.
35. Lists of provisions, dishes, pots, pans, tools, and spare parts common to prairie travelers may be found in Frederica B. Coons, *The Trail to Oregon* (Portland, 1954), 6-7, and Paden, 16.
36. The best description of the manufacture and maintenance of the emigrants' wagons is found in Stewart, 65 and 110-12.
37. At least one earlier marriage had taken place. On May 21, Parrish wrote: "Last night we had a wedding in camp. A Mr Martin Gillihan viz Mrs Asabel." Parrish, entry for May 21, 1844.
38. Pringle, p. 3.
39. Lavender, 217.
40. Minto, "Reminiscences," *OHQ,* II (1901), 146-47 and 150.
41. Parrish, entry for July 15, 1844.
42. *Ibid.,* entry for July 15; Minto, "Reminiscences," *OHQ,* II (1901), 151.
43. Charles L. Camp, ed., *James Clyman, Frontiersman . . . 1792-1881* (Portland, The Champoeg Press, 1960), 85-86.
44. Pringle, p. 4.
45. *Ibid.;* Catherine Sager Pringle, letter to Frederick Sager, December 21, 1854; Elizabeth Sager, letter to Frederick Sager, January 17, 1855, both in Helm, 82-95. While this might seem like a rare accident, year after year child after child fell under the wagon wheels. Parrish, entry for Sept. 22, 1844, described the same thing happening to his own daughter, Rebecca. See also Lavender, 375.
46. Little is known of Dr. Theophilos Dagon, also spelled Dagan and Dagin. Miles Cannon, *Waiilatpu, Its Rise and Fall, 1836-1847* (Boise, 1915), 75 and 82, states the doctor was married but for reasons of his own did not disclose why he came alone to Oregon. He was a skilled surgeon for his time and had a good education. He later settled at Oakland, Oregon, where he died at the age of 68. On learning of his death, Catherine Sager wrote: "For over a generation Dr. Dagon has lived in Oregon, having a large practice and embalming his name in memory but he has passed away in solitude without a friend to soothe his last hours or close his eyes in death. Ever green will his memory be in the heart of his children and the tear falls over the thought of his lonely death." From the Sager Collection of Mrs. Guy R. Carpenter. Mrs. Carpenter's files also include a letter by her aunt, Mrs. Naomi Hazlitt Swan: "He was as particular about the spelling of his name as we are about the spelling of ours and told Mother repeatedly that when she wrote him to spell it Dagon." Cannon is hereafter cited as *Waiilatpu.*
47. Parrish, entry for Aug. 1: "we rested here one day. These Indians are the Sues tribe. handsome & well behaved, moreso than any we have met with. This a.m. the Indians made a visit to our camp, men, women & children. With 5 of the most splendid Banners waving in the breas, a present of tobacco, Powder, lead, & other things were made them. Then the men sit down, & took a smoke. All out of the same hatchet pipe, in true indian stile. the Banners waving all the time." Crockett wrote in his diary: the Sioux "are evry way the netest and best looking indians that I ever saw. and is the strongest tribe in north america. they desired a present of which they got and then smoked the pipe of peace with our officers."
48. *Ibid.,* entry for August 15. Mrs. Seabren may have been Mrs. William Sebring, listed in "Roll of Oregon Pioneers Who Came to Oregon in 1844," OHS.
49. Camp, 97. The 1844 train was 50 days later in crossing the Continental Divide than were the American Board missionaries in 1836. The 1844 caravan had cause to be concerned.
50. Pringle, p. 4.
51. Minto, "Reminiscences," *OHQ,* II (1901), 163.
52. Elizabeth Sager to Uncle Frederick, Helm, 82-87.
53. Pringle, p. 5; Delaney, 7.
54. Fred Lockley, "Impressions and Observations of the Journal Man," MS,

extract on file, Whitman Mission NHS. Here Lockley was interviewing Lucretia Walker, whose father, John Perkins, was an 1844 emigrant and, later, was employed by Marcus Whitman.
55. Cannon, 77; Pringle to Uncle Frederick, Helm, 87-95; Nancy Osborn Jacobs, "Incidents of Early Western History, Pierce County," in *Told By the Pioneers*, I, 79-80.
56. Pringle, p. 5.
57. Minto, "Reminiscences," *OHQ*, II (1901), 166. Minto may be correct. It must be noted though that no other 1844 emigrant recalled seeing Carson — perhaps no one thought it important. Camp, 324n and 136, says that Jim Bridger was not at the fort when James Clyman arrived, having left on a trip to California.
58. Stewart, 16-17.
59. Pringle, p. 5.
60. *Ibid.*
61. Lockley, *Oregon Trail Blazers*, 326.
62. Delaney, 7-8.
63. Lockley, "Impressions and Observations of the Journal Man." It was at Pilgrim Springs, eight years earlier, that Narcissa Whitman almost lost her precious trunk when her husband wanted to throw it away because of its burden. Miles Cannon, "The Snake River in History," *OHQ*, XX (1919), 13.
64. Pringle, pp. 4-5. In her letter to Uncle Frederick, in Helm, 87-95, Catherine gave a slightly different version.
65. Cannon, *Waiilatpu*, 80.
66. Lockley, "Impressions and Observations of the Journal Man," quotes from an interview with Lucretia Walker, whose mother, Mrs. John Perkins, was one of the women who nursed the baby.
67. Pringle, p. 6.
68. Pringle to Uncle Frederick, Helm, 87-95.
69. Cannon, *Waiilatpu*, 78.
70. Pringle, p. 6.
71. *Ibid.*
72. Parrish, entry for October 3. "We are off by seven a. m. and arrived at Fort Boyce by one p. m. This fort is situat[*sic*] on the Lewis or Snake river."
73. Pringle, p. 6.
74. Parrish, entry for October 16 and 17. "Drove harde over the ruffest road yet, hills & Rocks, Awful."
75. Pringle, p. 6.
76. *Ibid.*, p. 7.
77. Parrish, entry for October 18. "so now we take our leave of this Blew Mountain never to travel it again. So here we are on the umatilla river with swarming of Indians around us; & Horses without *No*. The Indians are of the Kiuse tribes; they sold us Potatoes, and Pumpkins, & horses too. I traded, Bally, & Buck for a large bay horse, this morning."
78. Narcissa Whitman, letter, October 9, 1844, in *TOPA, 1893,* 68.
79. There is some confusion about dates. The Sager girls agreed that they left the Umatilla on October 17. Even by slow oxen this would have brought them to Waiilatpu by the 20th. However, Clifford M. Drury has discovered a letter in which Mrs. Whitman says the children arrived October 25; Drury, *Marcus Whitman, M. D.*, p. 355n. This latter is probably the correct date. Parrish, whose wagon was ahead of the Sagers', said he left the Umatilla for the mission on October 20. The Sagers probably left the river about the 22d. See, too, Pringle, p. 7.
80. Lockley, *Oregon Trail Blazers*, 327-28.
81. Pringle, p. 8. Drury, *Marcus Whitman, M. D.*, 356. When she came West in 1836, Narcissa Whitman thought western expressions very funny indeed. It is interesting to note that, eight years later, she used "yonder" so familiarly, if indeed, she did.

82. Pringle, p. 8. Lockley, *Oregon Trail Blazers,* 328-29. Lockley has a description by Elizabeth Sager Helm.
83. Elizabeth Sager to Uncle Frederick, in Helm, 82-87.
84. In 1840, the mountain man, Joe Meek, on his way to settle in Oregon, had persuaded the Whitmans to take his daughter, Helen Mar. She was a product of his mountain marriage to a Nez Perce. In 1841, another mountain man, Jim Bridger, did the same with one of his daughters, Mary Ann, also from a mountain marriage. In 1842, Narcissa Whitman herself took in a half-breed boy, David Malin, whose father had disappeared and whose mother, a Walla Walla Indian, had become a prostitute. Then, in 1843, Marcus Whitman, returning from his trip east, brought with him his 14-year-old nephew, Perrin Whitman.
85. Narcissa Whitman, letter, April 13, 1846, in *TOPA, 1893,* 79.
86. Sager Papers, Whitman College Library.
87. Narcissa Whitman, letter, April 13, 1846, in *TOPA, 1893,* 79.
88. Reprinted by permission of the publishers, The Arthur H. Clark Company, from *First White Women Over the Rockies* (3 vols., Glendale, 1963 and 1966), by Clifford M. Drury, I, 152. Drury quotes from a letter by Narcissa Whitman, April 2, 1846.
89. This chapter is a summary of Waiilatpu, 1836-44, based on the immense spadework of Clifford M. Drury in his various volumes on the missionaries, and Erwin N. Thompson, *Whitman Mission National Historic Site* (Washington, Government Printing Office, 1964).
90. Marcus Whitman, letter, May 10, 1839, in American Board of Commissioners for Foreign Missions Correspondence, copies at Whitman Mission NHS. Hereafter referred to as the ABCFM Correspondence.
91. Pierre Pambrun died from kicks from a horse in 1841. His replacement, Archibald McKinley, a Presbyterian, also became a close friend of the Whitmans.
92. The Cayuses spoke Nez Perce as well as their own language. Thus, the two missions found it convenient to conduct all preaching and teaching in the one tongue.
93. A notable exception was printing. Due perhaps to the Whitmans' preoccupation with other duties and their poor use of the Nez Perce language, the mission printing press was established at Lapwai. Rogers and Smith, assisted by the others, turned out the first works to be published in the Pacific Northwest. Thompson, 42-47.
94. Narcissa's state of mind during this bleak period is discussed in Erwin N. Thompson, "Narcissa Whitman: Woman, Wife, Mother, Missionary," *Montana Magazine,* XIII (1963), 15-27.
95. Whitman did not escape from all pettiness. At one time he got into a ridiculous argument with Asa Smith over some potatoes. Whitman was supposed to divide the potatoes between himself and Smith, but, according to Smith, he kept all the larger ones for himself and sent all the smaller ones to Smith.
96. The best description of this remarkable ride is in Drury, *Marcus Whitman, M.D.*
97. Marcus Whitman, letter, April 8, 1845, ABCFM Correspondence.
98. Nard Jones, *The Great Command, The Story of Marcus and Narcissa Whitman* (Boston, 1959), 297. Hereafter referred to as *The Great Command.*
99. Pringle, p. 10.
100. Delaney, 8.
101. Narcissa Whitman, letter, April 13, 1846, in *TOPA, 1893,* 79-80.
102. Pringle, p. 9.
103. *Ibid.,* p. 12.
104. Lockley, *Oregon Trail Blazers,* 330.
105. *Ibid.,* 345.
106. Pringle, p. 9. Narcissa Whitman's high opinion of Hinman is verified in a letter she wrote April 8, 1845, in *TOPA, 1893,* 70, "we have had an excellent teacher, a young man from New York." Later, Hinman became a teacher

at the Oregon Institute. Bancroft, I, 667n.
107. Pringle, pp. 10-11; Drury, *First White Women,* II, 315. Mary Walker expressed amazement and just a little concern over Catherine's forwardness when it came to praying in public. The Sagers discussed their religious training at the mission in Pringle, pp. 10-11; and Delaney, 8.
108. *Ibid.,* 12.
109. *Ibid.* Magpies were probably more troublesome than crows at Waiilatpu. They certainly are today.
110. *Ibid.*
111. Narcissa Whitman, letter, August 13, 1846, in *TOPA, 1893,* 81.
112. Delaney, 9. Emma Hobson was the motherless daughter of an 1843 immigrant. Her father left her and her sister with the missionaries until he got established in the Willamette.
113. Pringle, p. 12.
114. *Ibid.,* p. 9.
115. Narcissa Whitman, letter, Aug. 8, 1845, in *TOPA, 1893,* 184-86. Nearly all the material concerning this incident is drawn from this letter to the Methodist missionary, Mrs. Brewer, and from Pringle, p. 9. Netta S. Phelps, *The Valiant Seven* (Caldwell, 1945), 169, states, without citing an authority, that John Howard, another 1844 immigrant, was the person who persuaded Francis to leave. Howard was at Waiilatpu during the winter of 1844-45, employed as the mission blacksmith. In 1884, the Rev. J. S. Griffin told Matilda Sager's daughter, Bertha, that "he felt he had sent Francis Sager to his death. Francis had run away from the Whitman mission to the Willamette Valley because his teacher [Hinman] was so mean to him. Rev. Griffin found where Francis was working and reminded him of the promise made to his dying mother — that he would look after his sisters. Francis felt so deeply he became ill and vomited. He went back to the mission and . . . the Whitman massacre occurred." Notes in Matilda Sager Collection, Whitman College, Walla Walla, Wash.
116. Pringle, p. 12.
117. Narcissa Whitman, letter, Aug. 9, 1845, in *TOPA, 1893,* 184-85. In the same letter Mrs. Whitman referred to Hinman as "a good and faithful disciplinarian."
118. S. B. L. Penrose and S. B. L. Penrose, Jr., *Whitman Centennial Souvenir* . . . . (Walla Walla, no date), 22, quoting Catherine Sager Pringle.
119. J. E. Long, "Documents," *OHQ,* XI (1910), 312-13. The entry is in Clackamas County Probate Records, Book C, pp. 449-50. At that time the provisional government of the Oregon Country considered Waiilatpu to be in Clackamas County. Indeed, all the Columbia Plateau and southern British Columbia were included. See maps in Dorothy O. Johansen and Charles M. Gates, *Empire of the Columbia, A History of the Pacific Northwest* (New York, 1957), 299. J. W. Nesmith was also the outspoken leader of the anti-Jesuit group in Oregon. See Robert I. Burns, *The Jesuits and the Indian Wars of the Northwest* (New Haven, 1966), 167; "James Willis Nesmith," *Oregon Native Son,* I (Aug., 1899), 225-26; and Dumas Malone, *Dictionary of American Biography* (New York, Charles Scribner's Sons, 1943), VIII, 430-31.
120. Sager Papers, Whitman College, Walla Walla, Wash. A copy of a document in the Clackamas County Papers, Oregon State Archives, Salem, Ore.
121. Reprinted by permission of the publishers, The Arthur H. Clark Company, from *First White Women Over the Rockies,* by Clifford M. Drury, II, 280n. Garry was a Christian Indian of the Spokan tribe, having been educated at the Anglican mission at the Red River Settlement in Canada. He was somewhat of a disappointment to the American Board missionaries so far as being of assistance to them in their work. His story is told well in Thomas E. Jessett, *Chief Spokan Garry, 1811-1892* (Minneapolis, 1960).
122. Drury, *First White Women,* II, 279n, 288, and 288n.
123. Drury, *Marcus Whitman, M. D.*

124. It cannot be determined if Francis ran away before or after this meeting. If he had already left, it would seem likely that Mary Walker would have mentioned it in her diary. Since she is silent on the subject, Francis may still have been at home. All the mission was in attendance at the meeting except Mrs. Spalding.
125. Reprinted by permission of the publishers, The Arthur H. Clark Company, from *First White Women Over the Rockies*, by Clifford M. Drury, II, 281-82. The Sager descendants today believe that Francis and John already had been baptized in the Baptist church, to which both Henry and Naomi Sager had belonged. See also Pringle, p. 13. A letter from Mrs. Guy Carpenter to the writer quotes her uncle, Henry Hazlitt, a son of Matilda Sager, that neither John nor Francis took "kindly to the Presbyterianism of Dr. and Mrs. Whitman."
126. Narcissa Whitman, letter, November 26, 1846, reprinted by permission of the publishers, The Arthur H. Clark Co., from *First White Women*, by Drury, II, 295n. Narcissa used Rodgers as bait in her ceaseless but futile efforts to persuade her sister, Jane Prentiss, to come to Oregon. Jones, 291-92.
127. Eliza was the daughter of Henry and Eliza Spalding. She was a regular boarder at the mission school.
128. Cyrus Walker, "Occasional Address," *TOPA*, 1900, 39.
129. Drury, *First White Women*, II, 288 and 288n.
130. *Ibid.*, 318. Mary got back at Myra when the two ladies took all their children swimming in the summer of 1847. Someone in the Eells group did something "immodest" and Mrs. Walker had the pleasure of bringing it to Mrs. Eells's attention.
131. Reprinted by permission of the publishers, The Arthur H. Clark Company, from *First White Women Over the Rockies*, by Drury, II, 291n.
132. Narcissa Whitman, letter, July 17, 1846, in *TOPA, 1893*, 197.
133. *Ibid.*, letter, April 13, 1846, 80-81.
134. Matilda Sager Delaney and Cyrus Walker both tell this story. They disagree on many of the details but agree on one error, that the camping spot was where Walla Walla now stands. Walla Walla is but seven easy miles from the mission site and they would not have got away with staying an extra day for that short distance, which the writer has walked. Actually, their versions support strongly a site closer to the sawmill, which was 20 miles distant.
135. Delaney, 10. Mrs. Delaney believed in later years that Dr. Whitman had raced home from the Willamette just to take care of her. Although touching, it seems from Catherine's account that Matilda recovered before Whitman returned and that the doctor had not heard of her misfortune until he got home. Pringle, p. 13.
136. *Ibid.*
137. Narcissa was kept busy looking after the large family, yet there was always something missing. She wrote: "Henrietta, my baby, is a sweet, interesting child, and loves me as my own Alice used to, and I love her dearly; but that tender anxiety, so peculiar to mothers for their own offspring, is not for me to feel toward her, because it is impossible." Narcissa Whitman, letter, November 5, 1846, in *TOPA, 1893*, 204.
138. The Oregon Country south of the 49° parallel became American territory in 1846. This momentous event went almost unnoticed among the missionaries. They had been assured in their own minds for a long time that the southern part of the area would become American. Despite the Whitman-saved-Oregon myth, Marcus and his associates were not particularly interested where the diplomats finally established the boundary. In his correspondence, Whitman made it clear that he considered himself an important American pioneer and that he made a definite contribution to American settlement of the Oregon Country; but he claimed no more. Elkanah Walker, whose mission site at Tshimakain could conceivably have ended up on the British side of the line, only casually noted the settlement. He was indifferent to the boundary question and showed more concern about California, which he did not think the

United States was justified in taking from Mexico. See Elkanah Walker, letter to John Lee Lewes, January 13, 1847, in the Coe Collection of ABCFM Correspondence, Yale University, microfilm at Whitman Mission NHS.
139. Drury, *First White Women*, II, 313.
140. During her eleven years of married life, Mrs. Whitman watched her once-youthful figure grow to weigh more than 167 pounds. Narcissa Whitman, letter, October 9, 1844, in *TOPA, 1893*, 67.
141. Pringle, p. 19. Drury, *First White Woman*, II, 314-15.
142. *Ibid.*, II, 304 and 313n.
143. Pringle, p. 19. Tshimakain is as charming today as it was in 1847. The spring still flows, and quiet ranch buildings mark the site of the mission's structures.
144. Narcissa Whitman, letter, July 4, 1847, in *TOPA, 1893*, 215.
145. Drury, *Marcus Whitman, M. D.*, 361. Lockley, *Oregon Trail Blazers*, 330-31, quoting Elizabeth Sager.
146. Besides the short-lived Methodist missions that were begun in 1834 and the American Board missions started in 1836, there were the Catholic missions that did not get underway in Oregon until 1838. Vicar-General Francis N. Blanchet and Father Modeste Demers, both French Canadian priests, arrived at Fort Vancouver late that year. These two missionaries, later reinforced, established missions in what is now Washington State, both along the Columbia and in the Puget Sound area, and in the Willamette Valley of present-day Oregon. At almost the same time, Father Peter DeSmet, priest out of St. Louis, was establishing a string of missions in what is now northern Idaho and western Montana.

By 1842, the two Catholic endeavors had been united, and Francis Blanchet was designated bishop over the whole in 1844. In 1846 he was promoted to archbishop and Oregon was elevated to an ecclesiastical province. In 1847, his brother, A. M. A. Blanchet, was made bishop of Walla Walla, meaning the area about the Hudson's Bay post of Fort Walla Walla on the Columbia River. Blanchet arrived at the fort in September, much to the discomfort of the American Board missionaries. See Thompson, *Whitman Mission*, 53-56, including map.
147. After the massacre, Henry Spalding became convinced that the Catholic missionaries were responsible for the attack. So intense were his feelings that his mind was eventually deranged over the matter. Catherine Sager Pringle, in her reminiscences and correspondence, illustrated clearly that she was greatly influenced by Spalding's interpretation — as were many of Oregon's early Protestant settlers.
148. Clifford M. Drury has done the most careful analysis of the attack on the mission. See his various books on the American Board missions.
149. Pringle, pp. 16-17.
150. This aspect of Hill's career and his subsequent scouting for the American forces in California are admirably dealt with in David Lavender, *Land of Giants, The Drive to the Pacific Northwest, 1750-1950* (New York, 1958), 257-61.
151. Drury, *First White Women*, I, 163 and 163n.
152. Pringle, p. 22.
153. *Ibid.*, p. 30.
154. *Ibid.*
155. Mary Saunders, "The Whitman Massacre," MS, copy at Whitman Mission NHS.
156. Bancroft, I, 647n, says that L. Woodbury Saunders was a native of New Hampshire who had lived in both New York and Indiana. His wife, Mary Montgomery, was from Vermont.
157. Pringle, p. 39. Most published accounts state that Mrs. Hays had but one son, a four-year-old boy named Henry Clay. However, Catherine Pringle says there were two children when Mrs. Hays arrived, but that one of them died during the period of captivity.
158. Pringle, p. 21. J. S. Walker, "Ester Among the Cayuses, A True Tale of

1847," MS, typed copy at Whitman College Library.
159. Pringle, p. 31.
160. Penrose and Penrose, 24-25.
161. Pringle, p. 32.
162. There follow four different accounts of Francis Sager's death:
   1. Helm, *Lorinda Bewley*, 38-39. "Frank Sager then helped the school children to climb through a hole in the ceiling and hide in the attic, but in a short time Joe Lewis came and ordered them to come down. Frank did not come down with the others, and no doubt could have escaped — but he understood the Indian language, and hearing them say they were going to kill them all — he came down — and going to his beloved little sister Matilda — he put his arm around her and said — 'The Indians will kill me, but if you are spared, be a good girl, and meet me in heaven.' The children were lined up to be shot — an Indian jerked Frank out and Joe Lewis shot him."
   2. Pringle, letter to Frederick Sager, December 21, 1854, in Helm, *Lorinda Bewley*, 87-95. "They all climbed into the loft. When the Indians took the other children down he [Francis] stayed up there and had he only remained until night he might have escaped but his anxiety respecting his sister would not allow him to stay. He came down and the first thing he saw was his brother lying on the floor shot and his throat cut and his tippet stuffed into the wound. Francis pulled the tippet out. John tried to speak but died in the attempt. Francis burst into tears and taking his sister Matilda by the hand said 'I will soon follow my brother.' He was shot soon after by Joe Lewis."
   3. Eliza Spalding Warren, *Memoirs of the West* (Portland, 1916), 24-25. "the oldest boy, aged 18, was lying in a huddled heap, his throat cut from ear to ear, not yet dead. A younger brother, Francis, who was with us, stepped to his side and spoke his name. The dying boy tried to answer but could not speak. Francis said, 'I will soon be with you.'" "Francis Sager was standing between his sister Matilda and myself. They pulled him out a step or two and shot him. He fell at our feet. I was sure our time had come. I put my apron over my face. I did not want to see the guns pointed at us."
   4. Nathan Kimball, "Recollections of the Whitman Massacre," in *TOPA, 1903*, 192. "I saw him [Joe Lewis] take a boy about fifteen years old, named Sager, by the nose and shoot him in the head with a pistol."
163. When Kimball burst through the door, he shouted, "The Indians are killing us. I don't know what the damned Indians want to kill me for, I never did anything to them." Elizabeth Sager was so shocked to hear anyone say "damned" in front of Mrs. Whitman that she burst into giggles. See Drury, *First White Women*, I, 165.
164. Pringle, p. 32.
165. *Ibid.*
166. Any combat soldier is well acquainted with "the fog of battle" wherein no two accounts will agree in detail. Such is true of the accounts of the massacre written by the survivors. Nearly all these accounts were written many years later and dimmed memories further complicated them. An example of this is the four documents describing Francis Sager's death, above; another example is Narcissa's first wound. Few of those who wrote could bring themselves to say that this good woman was shot in the breast, and there is utter confusion whether she was shot in her left or right breast among those who dared. In order to describe the massacre with some degree of order, these minor disagreements have been omitted. However, all the primary sources have been checked point by point in compiling this version.
167. Pringle, p. 34.
168. E. M. Wilson, "The Last Day at Waiilatpu," *The Whitman College Quarterly*, I (1897), 26.
169. Pringle, p. 37.

170. *Ibid.*
171. Joseph Stanfield, a French Canadian, had been employed by Whitman. He lived in a lodge a short distance from the mission. Although several survivors of the massacre believed that Stanfield had encouraged the attack, it seems in the face of all the evidence that his only sins were the desire to live and his ability to get along with the Indians.
172. Elizabeth Sager, letter to Uncle Frederick, Helm, *Lorinda Bewley*, 82-87.
173. C. B. Bagley, *Early Catholic Missions in Oregon* (Seattle, 1932). Catherine Pringle was never to forget the burial. In 1882, she recounted that day in a letter to William H. Gray: "I will relate to you as near as I can the story of the burial. The indians did not intend to allow them to be buried but changed their notions and on Tuesday Jo Stanfield was set to digging a grave. This was dug on the foot of the Hill near where Dr. Whitman's child was buried. Was from two to three feet deep and wide enough to lay the bodies side by side. Wednesday Brouilette came and after getting his breakfast at the Old Mansion went to the Dr's house. The dead were lying where they fell. Domestic had been brought over from there and we were busy sewing it into sheets to wrap the corpses in. Jo Stanfield was washing the dead and as soon as we had a few sheets done the young women and girls took them over and as Jo wrapped them around the corpses they sewed them with needle and thread — I remained with my sick sisters who cried for me if I left them. I went over once to carry some sheets. Jo was washing Mrs. W. Brouiletts [*sic*] was lying [praying?] upon the table in the kitchen, I called his attention to Brother John who was lying on the floor. He looked around and told me to hush. I did not see him do anything to assist and I have asked others who were there all day and they said they did not see him do anything.

    "After they were all prepared they were put into an ox cart and hauled to the grave yard but not till after a run away of the team. If I recollect right the Priest went to the grave."

    From a letter dated Prineville, February 12, 1882, Sager Papers, Whitman College Library.
174. Lockley, *Oregon Trail Blazers*, 340.
175. Pringle, pp. 39-40 and 42. About this time, Joseph Stanfield tried to get Rebecca Hays to share his bed. Catherine insisted that Mrs. Hays refused Stanfield's overtures.
176. *Ibid.*, p. 51
177. *Ibid.*, pp. 41-42. Although Catherine avoided mentioning rape, there is little doubt but that it occurred.
178. *Ibid.*, p. 42.
179. Saunders, *ibid.* Pringle, p. 43. Catherine recounted that Mary Smith was taken by Edward's brother, "Clark".
180. Pringle, pp. 37-38.
181. Reprinted by permission of the publishers, The Arthur H. Clark Company, from *First White Women Over the Rockies*, by Drury, II, 325. The Eells and Walker families continued to live at Tshimakain and at the Hudson's Bay post of Fort Colville throughout the winter. But the Whitman massacre ended all hope of continuing the mission work. In the spring they were escorted out by the Oregon Volunteers. Both families continued to participate actively in the early history of the Oregon Country.
182. Pringle, pp. 40 and 43. Helm, *Lorinda Bewley*, 60-61.
183. Helm, *ibid.*, 51. Myra Sager Helm said it was Joseph Stanfield who came to Catherine's assistance; but Catherine said it was Nicholas Finley. Pringle, p. 45.
184. Pringle, p. 45.
185. *Ibid.*, p. 46.
186. *Ibid.*
187. *Ibid.*, p. 44.
188. Christmas was not observed at the Whitman mission; the missionaries con-

sidered it a holiday for Roman Catholics. At Tshimakain, the Walkers and the Eellses went so far as to let their children have a special lunch of cookies and milk on Christmas afternoons. If the Beardy episode actually happened on December 22, it illustrates how rapidly the Sagers' world was changing about them now that the Whitmans' influence was no longer present.
189. Pringle, pp. 44-45. The same story, in quite different detail, is told in W. D. Lyman, *An Illustrated History of Walla Walla County, State of Washington* (1901), 47-49. Lyman purports to be quoting Catherine — which he undoubtedly is, but with quite a lot of himself in it also.
190. John A. Hussey, *History of Fort Vancouver and Its Physical Structure* (Seattle, 1957), 85-87 and 93n.
191. A minority of settlers, including Governor Abernethy, hoped that a settlement could be reached without shedding more blood. This minority voice was not heard to any effective degree.
192. Pringle, p. 47.
193. Bancroft, I, 693-94.
194. Pringle, WMNHS, p. 36. See note 2.
195. Pringle, pp. 47-48. Edward tried to persuade Mary to stay, but he refused her suggestion that he go with her, fearing that the whites would shoot him. Later, a rumor spread in the Oregon Country that Mary Smith had been very much in love with Edward. Catherine denied this.
196. *Ibid.*, p. 47. There was at least one such scare while enroute to the fort, according to Catherine.
197. *Ibid.*, p. 48.
198. Helm, *Lorinda Bewley*, 72.
199. Catherine Pringle gave David a pocket testament before leaving Fort Walla Walla. She felt sure that the priests would take it from him. Pringle, p. 49.
200. James W. Nesmith in "Diary of the Emigration of 1843," *OHQ*, VII (1906), 356, describes this landmark in his entry for October 10: "Our camp is quite a picturesque place. Immediately under the high bluff of the far-famed Columbia, about one-half mile above are two rocks rising 100 feet above the level of the river. They are seperated by a small space, and are nearly round, presenting the appearance of two towers. Mr. McKinley informed me that the Indians looked upon them with a great deal of veneration, and say that they are two Indian damsels, petrified. I must confess that their appearance does not correspond very well with the tradition." Nesmith was too polite to say that the two rocks do look very much like the breasts of one Indian girl, petrified. Still standing, this dramatic formation has been repeatedly vandalized in recent years by spray-painting juveniles.
201. Jacobs, I, 86. Nancy was five years old when the Osborn family came west in 1845. She experienced the massacre, escaped with her father, and grew up to live a full life in Oregon. When she was quite old, in Portland, Oregon, she jumped through a second-story window to her death, screaming, "The Indians are coming to kill us." Letter to the writer from a descendant, Mrs. Ronald R. Smith, Van Nuys, Calif., 1962.
202. These sketches are still to be discovered. They were possibly destroyed in a disastrous fire at the Smithsonian Institution in 1865.
203. Helm, 73; Pringle, p. 49.
204. Drury, *First White Women*, I, 101.
205. Elizabeth Sager was certain that this was the reason for Spalding's disapproval. But James Douglas and Peter Skene Ogden were adherents to the Church of England. Most likely, Spalding did not distinguish between the two churches. Lockley, *Oregon Trail Blazers*, 342-43; Helm, 75-76; and Jones, 299. In an interview with Fred Lockley, Elizabeth Sager said that Henry Spalding believed that "Episcopalians were only one shade better than Catholics, and he didn't think any of them had any show of getting to heaven." She wanted to live with the Douglas family because "they had such good bread and cake, and the cutest beds for the children, that could be shoved right into the wall during the day." See *Walla Walla Union*, date

unknown, a clipping at Whitman College Library, Walla Walla, Wash.
206. Pringle, p. 49.
207. Lockley, *Oregon Trail Blazers,* 342-43. Catherine apparently was not at all upset by the sounds of guns. Pringle, p. 49.
208. Jacobs, I, 86. George Abernethy had arrived in Oregon in 1840, a member of Jason Lee's "Great Reinforcement" for the Methodist missions. After these missions came to an end, Abernethy became a merchant in the Willamette Valley. He is given credit as being the first merchant in the Oregon Country to establish credit and to set up direct business relations with New York firms. He died in 1877, an early example of a nativist American who looked upon the Roman Catholic Church as anti-American. He was a leader of men and a good man of that type that still causes a stir in a truly democratic society. See Arthur L. Throckmorton, "George Abernethy, Pioneer Merchant," *Pacific Northwest Quarterly, 48* (April, 1957), 76-88.
209. Pringle, p. 49.
210. Bancroft, I, 725.
211. Pringle, p. 50. Catherine names the five Cayuses as: Telapkait, Tamahas, Clokamus, Left Hand, and Wet Wolf. She was called upon to identify them after they were taken prisoners.
212. R. Ross Arnold, *Indian Wars of Idaho* (Caldwell, 1932), 98-101. A brief and different version of Lewis' death is in Myron Eells, *Marcus Whitman, Pathfinder and Patriot* (Seattle, 1909), 280.
213. Henry H. Spalding, letter, April 6, 1848, in *TOPA, 1893,* 101.
214. Lockley, *Oregon Trail Blazers,* 342-43.
215. This is the same publication that contained an article in the 1830's about the heathen tribes of the Oregon Country that were pleading for missionaries — the article that eventually led to the establishment of the Methodist and American Board missions.
216. These letters have been extensively quoted from in the preceding pages.
217. Clark Pringle was a private in the Oregon Volunteers in 1848. In his advanced years, he and Catherine enjoyed a monthly $12 pension for his services in revenging his future wife. Interview by the writer with Mrs. L. W. Armin, September, 1965. Also, Bancroft, I, 702n. The Pringle family and its arrival in Oregon is discussed in Morgan, I, 160-62.
218. Pringle, letter, December 25, 1881, Sager Papers, Whitman College.
219. *Ibid.,* letter, January 15, 1882.
220. *Ibid.,* letter, February 6, 1882.
221. *Ibid.,* letter, May 3, 1882.
222. *Ibid.,* letter, May 17, 1882.
223. *Ibid.,* letter to Myron Eells, no date.
224. Unidentified newspaper clipping, Catherine Pringle, in "gray" Scrapbook, p. 28, typed copy loaned by Mrs. Platz.
225. *Ibid.*
226. *Ibid.,* p. 11.
227. *Ibid.,* newspaper clipping, dated Walla Walla, October 24, 1897, in pink Scrapbook, loaned by Mrs. Platz.
228. *Ibid.,* Catherine Pringle, letter to *Spokesman-Review,* October 25, 1897.
229. William A. Mowry, *Marcus Whitman and the Early Days of Oregon* (New York, 1901), 234. "Mrs. Pringle's Address," *The Whitman College Quarterly,* I (1897), 30-31.
230. It has not been possible to resolve a simple contradiction here. Mowry, 232, states it was the marble slab for the great grave that had not arrived by November 29. *The Whitman College Quarterly,* I, (1897), 18-19, says it was the memorial shaft that was missing.
231. Wilson, *Whitman College Quarterly,* I, 18-19.
232. Elizabeth Sager, letter to Uncle Frederick, in Helm, 82-87. Josiah L. Parrish was still another Methodist minister.
233. Catherine Pringle and Elizabeth Sager, letters to their Uncle Frederick, in Helm, 82-95. Elizabeth wrote: "Brother John used to take me on his knee

and tell me over the names of my uncles and I distinctly remember Uncle Frederick's name, and this is all I know of my friends."
234. Elizabeth Sager Helm, letter to Myron Eells, Nencene, Jan. 26, 1890, Whitman College Library; Penrose and Penrose, 29.
235. Pringle, p. 50.
236. "Pioneer Families of the Oregon Territory, 1850," Oregon State Archives, Bulletin No. 30, *Publication No. 17,* 1951, p. 35; Linn County, Ore., 1850 Census, Sept. 17, 1850, p. 136, microfilm, Whitman College Library.
237. In a letter to the writer, Sept. 16, 1962, Mrs. L. W. Armin says that the family felt that way for a long time but, in more recent years, the Sager descendants are less concerned about Henrietta's acting career. On the other hand, Mrs. Guy Carpenter wrote in 1963: "Her uncle's family entertainment was hardly theater — merely singing, recitations, and dancing by his children and, for a short time, Aunt Henrietta who is said to have a good voice."
238. Letter to the writer, Oregon Historical Society, Aug. 31, 1965, citing the *Oregon Statesman* (Salem), Nov. 4, 1860. There was a John Cooper living in Linn County, Oregon, in 1850. Letter, Oregon Historical Society to Mrs. Guy Carpenter, July 28, 1960. Henrietta was living in Linn County at that time. In the Whitman College Library today is a letter from Catherine Pringle to Henry Spalding written in 1858. Catherine said that Henrietta was lost to them and to virtue because she was living with a man without benefit of marriage.
239. Matilda Delaney to Elizabeth, Oct. 29, 1862, Whitman College Library.
240. Catherine Pringle, letter, April, 1862, Whitman College Library.
241. Matilda Delaney, letter to Catherine and Elizabeth, July 19, 1863, Whitman College Library.
242. *Ibid.,* letter to Elizabeth, Nov. 21, 1864, Whitman College Library.
243. Matilda Delaney to Elizabeth, Nov. 5, 1865; and H. H. Spalding to "My Dear Daughter Henrietta," Oct. 25, 1866, both at Whitman College Library.
244. Catherine Pringle, letter, Sept. 28, 1868, Whitman College Library.
245. Lockley, *Oregon Trail Blazers,* 325-26. Letter from Oregon Historical Society to Mrs. Guy Carpenter, July 28, 1960, quoting an interview by the *Oregon Journal* with Elizabeth Sager Helm, July 25, 1923.
246. Maggie Sager Dockum, letter to Elizabeth Helm, December 4, 1877, and March 10, 1878, from copies on file, Oregon Historical Society, Portland, Oregon.
247. Lockley, *Oregon Trail Blazers,* 344-45.
248. Years later Matilda gave an interview to Fred Lockley that appears in his *Oregon Trail Blazers.* Lockley quotes Matilda as describing the discipline in the Geiger household as unusually severe. According to Lockley, Geiger tended to be sadistic when it came to beating Matilda — for potential as well as actual sins. There is nothing in Matilda's own account, *A Survivor's Recollections of the Whitman Massacre,* to support this version. Mrs. Guy Carpenter recalls her own mother as saying, "Mrs. Geiger was very young and, being from the South and used to colored help, expected more of Matilda than she should." While Matilda's life was severely governed and she was expected to perform many tasks, it would seem that Lockley may have overstressed the situation.
249. Lockley, *Oregon Trail Blazers,* 346.
250. *Ibid.*
251. Delaney, 29-30.
252. Lockley, *Oregon Trail Blazers,* 350.
253. Delaney, 29.
254. From photostat, "Guardian of Matilda Jane Sager," copy at Whitman College Library. This is an interesting document in that Geiger was the clerk of the probate court, Washington County, and signed this document that pertains to himself.
255. William Geiger, Jr., letter to Clark Pringle, May 21, 1855, Whitman College Library.

256. Matilda Sager to her sisters, May 20, 1855, Whitman College Library.
257. Pringle, letter to Uncle Frederick, December 21, 1855, in Helm, *Lorinda Bewley*, 87-95. Clifford M. Drury, *Elkanah and Mary Walker, Pioneers Among the Spokanes* (Caldwell, 1940), 235.
258. Matilda Delaney to Elizabeth, Oct. 29, 1862, Whitman College Library.
259. *Ibid.*, June 18, 1863.
260. Matilda Delaney to Catherine and Elizabeth, Nov. 21, 1864, Whitman College Library.
261. Matilda Delaney to Elizabeth, Mar. 3, 1864, Whitman College Library.
262. *Ibid.*, Aug. 14, 1863.
263. *Ibid.*, Nov. 5, 1865.
264. Matilda Delaney to Catherine, Nov. 25, 1865, Whitman College Library. Matilda and Matthew were married January 18, 1866, by the Reverend Robert McCulloch. Copies of the marriage certificate and license at Whitman College Library.
265. Matilda Delaney to Elizabeth, Nov. 15, 1868. Catherine also saw Dr. Dagon that summer when he came to visit her. Catherine Pringle, letter to Henry Spalding, Sept. 28, 1868, Whitman College Library.
266. Matilda Delaney to Elizabeth, Feb. 6, 1876, Whitman College Library.
267. David Delaney came to Oregon in 1845, his parents having preceded him by two years. He first settled near Salem. In 1883 he moved to Washington Territory where he settled near Farmingham, just one year after the Fultzes. His first wife, Jane Edgar, died in 1885. Delaney was a strong Republican. One wonders if Matilda followed his politics or followed her own strong Democratic heart.
268. Copy of marriage certificate, Whitman College Library.
269. *Walla Walla Journal*, Sept. 19, 1888.
270. More likely this sister was Catherine who appears to have been closer to her, both spiritually and physically, than Elizabeth, although all three remained remarkably close in their feelings toward one another. Delaney, 42.

Bibliography

Manuscript Material

While it has been possible only to trace the lives of the Sagers, particularly the adult years of the four girls who survived the Whitman massacre, a large amount of manuscript material in several depositories came to light during the research.

1. *Whitman Mission National Historic Site, Washington.* This National Park's history files contain photostatic and typed copies of a large collection of the American Board's mission correspondence. Particularly useful were letters by Marcus and Narcissa Whitman from the arrival of the Sagers in 1844 until the massacre in 1847. The Park also has, on microfilm, the Coe Collection of mission correspondence, the originals of which are at the Yale University Library, New Haven, Conn. Of importance in the Park's files is a typed copy of the memories of Mary Saunders, titled "The Whitman Massacre." Mrs. Saunders was at the mission in the fall of 1847. Also useful was a typed extract from Fred Lockley, "Impressions and Observations of the Journal Man," October 17, 1930.

2. Three descendants of the Sagers have provided considerable original material, supported by both correspondence and conversations: Mrs. Guy Carpenter, San Francisco, Calif.; Mrs. L. W. Armin, Sioux Falls, S. D.; and Mrs. Harry W. Platz, Seattle, Wash. Mrs. Carpenter is a granddaughter of Matilda Sager Delaney; Mrs. Armin and Mrs. Platz are granddaughters of Catherine Sager Pringle. All three have maintained a deep interest in the Sager family.

3. *Penrose Library, Whitman College, Walla Walla, Wash.* The Whitman College Library proved a lodestone for manuscripts and photographs concerning the Sagers. Of great help were the Catherine Sager Pringle Papers, the William H. Gray Papers, the Matilda Sager Delaney Papers, and a collection listed simply as the "Sager Papers." Also of help was J. S. Walker, "Ester Among the Cayuses, A True Tale of 1847." Important too was the unusual letter by Henry Spalding to Henrietta Sager, Oct. 25, 1886. Permission to quote herein from these has been granted by the library.

4. *Oregon Historical Society, Portland, Ore.* From its wealth of manuscript material on pioneer days, the Oregon Historical Society was able to provide the answers to many puzzling questions, and always with speed and accuracy.

5. *Idaho Historical Society, Boise, Idaho.* Among its manuscript collections, this Society has the most valuable diary of Edward Evans

Parrish, "E. E. Parrish's Traveling Diary Across the Plains," which described his journey over the Oregon Trail in 1844. This was one of the few diaries kept that year. The IHS has granted permission to quote the diary herein.

6. *Account by Catherine Sager Pringle.* Copies of this account are located in various depositories. The original manuscript is at Whitman College Library. (Quoted herein with permission.) Edmond S. Meany made copies of this manuscript and placed them in the Library, University of Washington, Seattle. In 1954, Mrs. Celista C. Platz, a granddaughter of Catherine Sager Pringle, typed the Meany copy on stencils. I used this mimeographed copy (checked against the original at Whitman College) throughout — with one or two exceptions which are marked. These exceptions were taken from a copy of Mrs. Pringle's account in the Seattle Public Library. The origin of this latter version is unknown. The main difference between it and the Meany copy is that of style and construction rather than fact. It is probable that Catherine's very first draft, not made available to Meany, contained more anti-Catholic sentiments than her final version.

Periodicals and Articles
Bright, Verne, "The Folklore and History of the 'Oregon Fever'," *Oregon Historical Quarterly,* LII (1951), 241-53.
Cannon, Miles, "The Snake River in History," *OHQ,* XX (1919), 1-23.
Carstensen, Vernon, "Diary of Samuel Black Crockett, 1844," in Washington State Historical Society, *Building a State: Washington, 1889-1939,* Tacoma, 1940, 594-607.
Dale, Harrison C., "The Organization of the Oregon Emigration Companies," *OHQ,* (1915), 205-27.
Deady, Matthew P., "The Annual Address," *Transactions of the... Oregon Pioneer Association,* 1876.
Drury, Clifford M., "The Columbia Maternal Association," *OHQ,* XXXIX (1938), 99-122.
Flora, S. D., "The Great Flood of 1844 along the Kansas and Marais des Cygnes Rivers," *Kansas Historical Quarterly,* 20 (1952), 73-81.
Fenton, William D., "The Winning of the Oregon Country," *OHQ,* VI (1905), 343-78.
"James Willis Nesmith," *Oregon Native Son,* I (Aug., 1889), 225-26.
Kimball, Nathan, "Recollections of the Whitman Massacre," *TOPA,* 1903.
Lockley, Fred, "Reminiscences of Mrs. Frank Collins, nee Martha Elizabeth Gilliam," *OHQ,* XVII (1916), 358-72.
Long, J. E., "Documents," *OHQ,* XI, (1910), 312-13.
Lyman, W. D., "Reminiscences of Wm. M. Chase," *OHQ,* I (1900), 269-95.
Minto, John, "Reminiscences of Honorable John Minto, Pioneer of 1844," *OHQ,* II, (1901), 119-67, 209-54.

Minto, John, "Antecedents of the Oregon Pioneers and the Light These Throw on their Motives," *OHQ*, V (1904), 38-63.
Minto, John, "Robert Wilson Morrison," *TOPA, 1894.*
"Mrs. Nancy Morison, the Oregon Pioneer Woman," *TOPA, 1890.*
Nesmith, James W., "Diary of the Emigration of 1843, *OHQ*, VII (1906), 329-59.
Pringle, Catherine Sager, "Mrs. Pringle's Address," *Whitman College Quarterly*, I (1897), 30-31.
"Reminiscences of Washington Smith Gilliam," *TOPA, 1903.*
Shaw, T. C., "Capt. William Shaw," *TOPA, 1887.*
Spalding, Henry H., Correspondence in *TOPA, 1893.*
Thompson, Erwin N., "Narcissa Whitman: Woman, Wife, Mother, Missionary," *Montana Magazine of History*, 12 (1963), 15-27.
Throckmorton, Arthur L., "George Abernethy, Pioneer Merchant," *Pacific Northwest Quarterly*, 48 (April, 1957), 76-88.
Walker, Cyrus, "Occasional Address," *TOPA, 1900.*
Wilson, Mrs. E. M., "The Last Day at Waiilatpu," *Whitman College Quarterly*, I (1897), 17-28.
Wyman, Walker D., "Western Folklore and History," *American West*, I (1897), 44-51.
Young, F. G., "The Oregon Trail, *OHQ*, I (1900), 339-70.

Books and Pamphlets
Arnold, R. Ross, *Indian Wars of Idaho*, Caldwell, 1932.
Bagley, C. B., *Early Catholic Missions in Oregon*, Seattle, 1932.
Bancroft, Hubert Howe, *Works*, Vols. 29 and 30, *History of Oregon*, San Francisco, Vol. 29, 1886; Vol. 30, 1888.
Billington, Ray Allen, *The American Frontier*, Washington, Service Center for Teachers of History, Publication No. 8.
Billington, Ray Allen, *The Far Western Frontier, 1830-1860*, New York, 1956.
Bining, Arthur Cecil, *A History of the United States*, New York, 1950.
Bureau of the Census, U. S. Department of Commerce, *Historical Statistics of the United States, Colonial Times to 1957*, Washington, 1961.
Burns, Robert I., *The Jesuits and the Indian Wars of the Northwest*, New Haven, 1966.
Camp, Charles L. ed., *James Clyman, Frontiersman . . . 1792-1881*, Portland, 1960.
Cannon, Miles, *Waiilatpu, Its Rise and Fall, 1836-1847*, Boise, 1915.
Coons, Frederica B., *The Trail to Oregon*, Portland, 1954.
Delaney, Matilda Sager, *A Survivor's Recollection of the Whitman Massacre*, Spokane, 1920.
Drury, Clifford M., *Marcus Whitman, M.D., Pioneer and Martyr*, Caldwell, 1937.
Drury, Clifford M., *Elkanah and Mary Walker, Pioneers among the Spokanes*, Caldwell, 1940.

Drury, Clifford M., *First White Women Over the Rockies, Diaries, Letters, and Biographical Sketches of the Six Women of the Oregon Mission*, 3 volumes, Glendale, Vols. I & II, 1963; Vol. III, 1966.
Eells, Myron, *Marcus Whitman, Pathfinder and Patriot*, Seattle, 1909.
Federal Writers' Project, WPA, *The Oregon Trail, The Missouri River to the Pacific Ocean*, New York, 1939. American Guide Series.
Gay, Theresa, *James W. Marshall, The Discoverer of California Gold, A Bibliography*, Georgetown, Calif., 1967.
Ghent, W. J., *The Road to Oregon, A Chronicle of the Great Emigrant Trail*, New York, 1929.
Gray, William H., *A History of Oregon*, Portland, 1870.
Helm, Myra Sager, *Lorinda Bewley and the Whitman Massacre*, Portland, 1951.
Hussey, John A., *History of Fort Vancouver and Its Physical Structure*, Seattle, 1957.
Jacobs, Nancy Osborn, "Incidents of Early Western History, Pierce County," in *Told by the Pioneers*, Vol. I, 1937.
Jessett, Thomas E., *Chief Spokan Garry, 1811-1892; Christian, Statesman, and Friend of the White Man*, Minneapolis, 1960.
Johansen, Dorothy O. and Charles M. Gates, *Empire of the Columbia, A History of the Pacific Northwest*, New York, 1957.
Jones, Nard, *The Great Command, The Story of Marcus and Narcissa Whitman and the Oregon Country Pioneers*, Boston, 1959.
Lavender, David, *Land of Giants, The Drive to the Pacific Northwest, 1750-1950*, New York, 1958.
Lavender, David, *Westward Vision, The Story of the Oregon Trail*, New York, 1963.
Lockley, Fred, *Oregon Trail Blazers*, New York, 1929.
Lyman, W. D., *An Illustrated History of Walla Walla County, State of Washington*, n. p., 1901.
Morgan, Dale, ed., *Overland in 1846, Diaries and Letters of the California-Oregon Trail*, 2 volumes, Georgetown, Calif., 1963.
Nebraska State Historical Society, *Publications*, Vol. 20.
Oregon State Archives, "Pioneer Families of the Oregon Territory, 1850," Bulletin No. 3, *Publication No. 17*.
Paden, Irene, *Wake of the Prairie Schooner*, New York, 1947.
Penrose, S. B. L. and S. B. L. Penrose, Jr., *Whitman Centennial Souvenir, At Waiilatpu, Impressions and Recollections of Visitors to the Whitman Mission, 1836-1847*, Walla Walla, n. d.
Phelps, Netta Sheldon, *The Valiant Seven*, Caldwell, 1945.
Stewart, George R., *The California Trail*, New York, 1962.
Thompson, Erwin N., *Whitman Mission National Historic Site*, Washington, 1964. National Park Service Historical Handbook Series No. 37.
Warren, Eliza Spalding, *Memoirs of the West*, Portland, 1916.

INDEX

Abernethy, George, 123, 124, 128
Abernethy, William, 138
Alaska, 115
Alleghenies, 1
American Board of Commissioners for Foreign Missions, 43, 44, 45, 46, 47, 54, 55, 57, 59, 72, 74, 80, 84, 136
American Board missionaries, 7, 41, 115
Armin, Sadie Collins, 138
"Aunt Sally" (see Shaw, Mrs. Wm.)

Bancroft, H. H., 10, 133, 134
Bath, N.Y., 46
Bear River Divide, 27
Beardy, 113, 114, 117
Bewley, Crocket, 90, 91, 101, 110
Bewley, Lorinda, 90, 108, 109, 110, 117, 124
Big Muddy Creek, 27
Big Sandy, 24
Bitterroots, 127
Black's Fork, 26
Black Hawk War, 10
Blanchet, A.M.A., 82, 136
Blue Mountains, 23, 31, 35, 36, 49, 51, 62, 74, 77, 80, 85, 89, 92
Boise River, 33
Boston, Mass., 41, 57
Brewer, Mrs. William H., 69
Bridger, Jim, 26, 44
Bridger, Mary Ann, 73, 91, 95, 105, 124
Brouillet, J.B.A., 92, 106, 107, 136
Brownsville, Ore., 144
Burnett, Peter H., 30
Burnt River, 33

Calapooia River, 140
California, 7, 8, 12, 72, 73, 83, 84, 86, 102, 115, 138, 139, 142, 143, 145, 147, 148, 150, 152
Canada, 86
Canfield, W. D., 90, 93, 102
Cannon, Miles, 31
Capler's Landing, 7, 8
Carney, Catherine, 2
Carney, Naomi (see Sager, Naomi)
Carson, Kit, 26, 84
Cascades, 121, 125
Catholic Church, 134
Catholic mission, 92
Catholic missionaries, 82, 92

Cave, Reverend James, 16, 42
Cayuses, 36, 48, 49, 50, 72, 75, 79, 80, 81, 82, 83, 84, 85, 86, 87, 88, 90, 91, 97, 99, 101, 103, 104, 108, 110, 111, 115, 116, 117, 119, 125, 126, 127, 128
Chimney Rock, 19
Cincinnati, Ohio, 46
Clearwater River, 49, 54
Clyman, James, 18
Coeur d'Alenes, 127
Collins, Lucia Pringle, 138
Columbia Gorge, 65, 121
Columbia River, 4, 10, 33, 37, 49, 50, 54, 62, 73, 79, 80, 86, 115, 118, 119, 122, 123, 125
Condon, Brother, 144
Continental Divide, 23, 48
Cooper, Jno. L., 143, 145
Cooper, Mrs. Jno. L. (see Sager, Henrietta)
Cornwall, Rev. J. A., 147
Cottonwood, Calif., 148, 150
Council Bluffs, 7
Court House Rock, 19
Craig, William, 111

Dagon, Dr., 21, 26, 27, 31, 32, 33, 35, 36, 39, 40, 152
Daniel, Wyo., 48
Daniels, Mrs., 31
Delaney, David, 153
Delaney, Mrs. David (see Sager, Matilda)
Devil's Gap, 23
Dockum, Maggie Sager, 145
Donner tragedy, 78
Douglas, James, 115, 123
Douglas, Mrs., 123

Eads, Clark, 14, 15
Eads, Mrs., 31, 42
Eads, Solomon, 71, 72
Edward (Tiloukaikt's son), 110, 111, 112, 117
Eells, Cushing, 41, 42, 53, 55, 57, 78, 79, 126, 134, 148
Eells, Myron, 140
Eells, Myra, 53, 76, 150
Emigrant House, 91, 101, 105, 106, 107, 117

Fairfield, N.Y., 43, 47
Farewell Bend, 33
Farmington, Wash., 152, 153
Finley, Nicholas, 87, 88, 90, 112
Five Crows, 109, 117
Flatheads, 45, 127
Ford, Nathaniel, 7

[174]

Ford wagon train, 18, 23
Forest Grove, Ore., 146, 148
Fort Boise, 33, 49, 54
Fort Bridger, 22, 26, 27
Fort Hall, 7, 27, 86, 114
Fort Laramie, 13, 21, 23
Fort Vancouver, 49, 114, 115, 116, 122, 123
Fort Walla Walla, 49, 51, 54, 65, 73, 82, 102, 103, 104, 106, 114, 116, 117, 118, 119, 121
Fort Waters, 126
Francis (Indian), 110
Franklin Academy, 46
Frémont, John C., 26, 84, 86
Frost, Mrs., 23
Fultz, Ida Leona, 152
Fultz, Matthew, 152, 153
Fultz, Mrs. Matthew (*see* Sager, Matilda)

Garry, Spokan, 73
Geiger, William, Jr., 146, 147, 148, 149, 152
Geiger, Mrs. William, 147
Gilliam, Cornelius, 10, 11, 15, 17, 18, 123, 126
Gilliland, Isaac, 90, 97
Grande Ronde, 35, 36
Grant, Richard "Johnny," 27, 30
Grant, U. S., 71
Gray, William H., 46, 47, 48, 51, 53, 55, 57, 73, 91, 131, 133, 134
Great Grave, 125, 128, 131, 134, 137, 140
Great Migration, 4, 57, 71
Great Philadelphia Wagon Road, 1
Great Register of the Desert, 23
Green Point, 124
Green River, 24, 25, 44, 48
Greene, Rev. Samuel, 136
Griffin, Mr., 148

Hall, Peter, 90, 101, 102, 115
Hall, Mrs. Peter, 98, 99, 112
Harris, Moses "Black," 7
Hart, Eliza, 46
Hart, Horace, 119
Hawaii, 146
Hays, Henry Clay, 91
Hays, Rebecca, 90, 91, 98, 99, 117
Hazlitt, Hays, 152
Hazlitt, Henry, 152
Hazlitt, Lewis Mackey, 148, 149, 150, 151, 152
Hazlitt, Mrs. Lewis (*see* Sager, Matilda)
Helm, Mary, 140

Helm, William Fletcher, 140
Helm, Mrs. Wm. Fletcher (*see* Sager, Elizabeth)
Henley, Calif., 143, 150, 151, 152
Hill, Tom, 82, 83, 84, 86
Hillsboro, 148
Hinman, Alanson, 62, 68, 69, 70, 73, 74, 76, 88, 121
History of Oregon, 134
History of the Northwest Coast, 133
Hoffman, Jacob, 90, 97, 98
Horse Creek, 44
Howland, Mrs., 138
Hudson's Bay Co., 10, 27, 33, 45, 49, 51, 88, 114, 115, 116, 123, 124, 136
Hushus Muk Muk (Yellow Head), 75

Idaho, 45, 128, 131
Illinois, 89
Independence, Mo., 4, 7, 18
Independence Rock, 23
Indian Room, 91
Indiana, 2
Iowa, 71
Istulest, 112

Jackson, Mr., 119
Johnson, Mary, 119, 146
Johnson, Mrs. William, 138
Joseph, Chief, 83

Kamiah, 54
Kansas River, 12, 23
Kees, Monroe, 142
Kensington, Conn., 47
Kentucky, 10
Kimball, Nathan, 90, 93, 98, 99, 101, 104
Kimball, Susan, 110
Kindred, John, 16
King, Mr., 93
King, Mary, 16

Lancaster Co., Pa., 1
Lane Theological Seminary, 46
Lapwai, 51, 54, 57, 78, 88, 111, 119
Lapwai Creek, 49, 50, 102, 107, 119
Laramie Mountains, 19
Lee, Jason, 45
Lewis, Joe, 86, 87, 90, 97, 98, 99, 104, 128
Lewis and Clark, 50
Lewiston, 13, 144, 155
Liberty, Mo., 44, 46
Lincoln, Abraham, 151, 152
Linn County, 142

[175]

Little Muddy Creek, 27
Looking Glass, Chief, 83
Loudoun Co., Va., 1
Lovettsville, Va., 1

McBean, William, 102, 103, 115, 118, 119, 121
McBean, Mrs., 119
McKinley, Archibald, 73
McLoughlin, John, 49, 115
Magruder, Edmund B., 71, 72
Maine, 86
Malin, David, 103, 106, 121
Manson, David, 88
Marsh, Mary, 117
Marsh, William, 90, 97
Marshall, James W., 12
Marysville, Calif., 144
Meek, Helen Mar, 40, 59, 91, 98, 105, 110, 111, 127, 133
Meek, Joseph, 110, 127, 128
Methodist, 45, 63, 130
Methodist missionaries, 41
Mexican Territory, 27
Mexican War, 86
Mill Creek, 77
Minto, John, 11, 12, 25
Missouri, 3, 10, 24, 41, 70, 71, 89
Missouri River, 4, 5, 7, 8, 9, 58, 124
Montana, 45
Monterey, 146
Morrison, Robert Wilson, 11, 12, 18
Morrison, Mrs., 13
Morrison's Company, 23
Mr. P., 68, 69
Munger, Asahel, 53

Nemaha Indian Agency, 9, 12
Nemaha River, 13, 14
Nesmith, James W., 70, 71
New Brunswick, Canada, 70
New Jersey, 129
New Jerusalem Lutheran Church, 1
New York, 43, 45, 46, 145
Nez Percés, 45, 48, 49, 50, 51, 54, 82, 83, 111, 119, 127
Nichols, Benjamin, 71, 72
Nichols, John, 23
Nichols, Mrs. John, 31
North Carolina, 10
North Fork (Platte River), 18

Odenwald, Hessen, 1
Ogden, Peter Skene, 114, 115, 116, 117, 118, 119, 121, 123, 124
Ohio, 142, 145
Ohio Valley, 1

Ontario, Canada, 43
Oregon, 3, 4, 7, 8, 9, 13, 24, 36, 41, 42, 45, 46, 48, 49, 55, 70, 71, 74, 78, 79, 82, 115, 119, 123, 124, 128, 129, 131, 136, 139, 142, 144, 155
Oregon City, Ore., 41, 42, 124, 127
Oregon Institute, 139
Oregon Pioneer and Historical Society, 134, 155
Oregon Trail, 4, 22, 30, 35, 48, 49, 51, 54, 77, 85, 97, 113, 125, 131, 145, 152
Oregon Volunteers, 123, 126, 128
Osborn, Josiah, 89, 90, 101, 102, 115, 121
Osborn, Mrs. Josiah, 91, 92, 103
Osborn, Nancy, 90, 121
Osborn, Salvijane, 90, 91, 92

Pacific Coast, 5
Pacific Northwest, 54, 57, 128, 131, 134
Pacific Ocean, 23
Palouse hills, 79
Pambrun, Pierre, 49, 51
Parker, Samuel, 43, 44, 45, 46, 48
Parrish's Gap, 138
Parrish, E. E., 14, 17, 18, 138, 142
Parrish, Josiah L., 139
Parrish, Mrs., 139
Pendleton, Ore., 36
Penrose, S. B. L., 140
Perkins, 42
Peupeumoxmox, 83
Philadelphia, 1
Picard, Mrs. C. J., 134
Pilgrim Springs, 30
Pittsburg, Pa., 11
"Place of the Rye Grass" (see Waiilatpu)
Platte Co., Mo., 3
Platte River, 7, 12, 13, 16, 18
Portland, Ore., 123, 140, 155
Powder River, 35
Prattsburg, N.Y., 45
Prentiss, Narcissa (see Whitman, Narcissa)
Price, Hannah, 2
Prineville, Ore., 133
Pringle, Catherine (see Sager, Catherine)
Pringle, Clark Spencer, 130, 131, 142, 143, 148, 149

Quakers, 1

Red Bluff, Calif., 145
Reseda, Calif., 155
Roberts, William M., 129

Roberts, Mrs. William M., 129, 142
Robb, Jacob, 138, 139
Robidoux, Joseph, 4, 5
Robinson, Emma, 67
Rocks of the Cayuse Girls, 121
Rocky Mountains, 13, 18, 24, 48, 82
Rodgers, Andrew, 74, 75, 76, 79, 84, 88, 98, 99, 102, 111, 140
Rogers, Cornelius, 53
Rushville, N.Y., 43

Sacramento, Calif., 143
Sacramento River, 73
Sager, Catherine, 2, 3, 8, 9, 12, 13, 16, 18, 19, 21, 24, 25, 26, 27, 30, 31, 33, 39, 40, 41, 59, 60, 61, 62, 63, 65, 68, 71, 74, 75, 78, 79, 83, 84, 86, 93, 101, 103, 104, 105, 108, 110, 111, 112, 113, 114, 119, 121, 122, 123, 124, 129, 130, 131, 133, 134, 136, 137, 138, 139, 140, 142, 143, 144, 145, 148, 153, 155
Sager, Christian, 1
Sager, Della, 143, 144
Sager Dramatic Troupe, 142, 143
Sager, Elizabeth M., 2, 21, 26, 27, 30, 31, 33, 39, 41, 61, 63, 65, 71, 75, 76, 93, 103, 104, 105, 106, 107, 111, 119, 122, 123, 124, 129, 130, 136, 138, 139, 140, 143, 144, 145, 148, 151, 152
Sager, Francisco (Francis), 2, 22, 26, 35, 36, 39, 40, 41, 61, 62, 63, 65, 67, 68, 69, 70, 71, 73, 78, 95, 97, 98, 105, 111, 124, 137
Sager, Frederick, 129, 139
Sager, George, 1
Sager, George, Jr., 1
Sager, Heinrich (Henry), 1, 2, 3, 4, 5, 10, 11, 13, 14, 16, 18, 21, 24, 25, 26, 30, 31, 41, 48, 59, 71, 72, 80, 90, 110, 123, 124, 129, 155
Sager, Henrietta Naomi, 31, 41, 60, 71, 76, 103, 108, 122, 123, 124, 129, 130, 136, 139, 142, 143, 144, 145, 148, 150
Sager, John C., 2, 22, 26, 27, 31, 39, 40, 41, 61, 62, 68, 69, 70, 71, 73, 77, 78, 79, 80, 95, 97, 98, 99, 105, 111, 113, 124, 137, 142
Sager, Louise (Hannah Louise), 4, 26, 31, 35, 40, 41, 60, 61, 70, 71, 91, 98, 103, 105, 110, 111, 124, 133, 140
Sager, Matilda Jane, 2, 26, 31, 41, 59, 61, 63, 65, 71, 77, 78, 95, 97, 103, 124, 131, 139, 143, 144, 146, 147, 148, 149, 150, 151, 152, 153, 155
Sager, Naomi, 2, 4, 5, 13, 14, 15, 16, 18, 19, 24, 25, 26, 27, 30, 31, 48, 59, 60, 124, 155
Sager, Rosanna L. (*see* Sager, Henrietta)
Sager, Solomon, 142, 143
Salem, Ore., 129, 138, 139, 142
Sales, Amos, 90, 91, 101, 110
Salmon Falls, 30
San Francisco, Calif., 143, 144, 150, 151
Saunders, L. W., 88, 90, 95, 97
Saunders, Mary, 88, 113, 117
Saxton, C., 41
Scotts Bluff, 19
Seabren, Mrs. Susan, 23
Seattle, Wash., 131
Seeger (*see* Sager), 1
Seling, William, 42
Seminole War, 10
Seneca, Kansas, 13
Shaw, William, 10, 11, 13, 18, 25, 30, 31, 32, 33, 35, 37, 39, 40, 41, 42, 59, 70, 71, 72, 80, 123
Shaw, Mrs. William, 13, 25, 31, 39
Shaw's Company, 21, 23, 26, 33, 35
Sierra Nevada, 78
Simmons, Michael, 10, 17
Shover, Maria Elizabeth, 1
Smith, Alvin T., 146
Smith, Asa, 53, 55, 57, 73
Smith, Joseph, 89, 107, 110, 112, 124
Smith, Mary, 110, 111, 112, 117, 119
Smith, Sarah, 53
Snake River, 7, 26, 30, 32, 33, 49, 50, 54, 79, 126
Solomon, 111, 121
South Fork (Platte River), 18
South Pass, 23, 48
Spalding, Eliza, 24, 46, 48, 49, 51, 75, 119
Spalding, Eliza (daughter), 88, 107, 111, 117, 119
Spalding, Henry, 7, 46, 47, 49, 50, 55, 57, 73, 83, 88, 92, 93, 102, 107, 111, 119, 123, 129, 134, 136, 143, 144, 146

Spokane, Wash., 131, 138
Spokane River, 79
Spokans, 54, 72
Spokesman-Review, 136
St. Joseph, Mo., 4, 5, 7, 9, 13
St. Joseph train, 18
Stanfield, Joseph, 90, 105, 106, 107, 110, 112, 117, 124, 126
Stanley, John Mix, 121, 122, 123, 150
Stephens-Townsend-Murphy Party, 7
Sterling, Mr., 145
Stickus, 92, 93, 117
Sutter, John A., 72
Sutter's Fort, 73, 75, 146
Sweagle, 131
Sweetwater River, 23

Tamsucky, 99
Temi (*see* Whitman, Alice Clarissa)
Tewat, 85, 86, 87, 103
The Dalles, 69, 79, 88, 105, 115, 121, 144
Thornton, Mrs. J. Quinn, 129, 142, 146
Thorp, John, 7
Three Island Crossing, 30, 32
Tiloukaikt, 95, 97, 110, 111, 127
Tomahas, 75, 83, 95, 97, 127
Tshimakain, 41, 42, 54, 55, 57, 59, 72, 78, 79, 110, 121, 126, 138, 150
Tucannon River, 54

Umatilla River, 36, 37, 39, 42, 74, 92, 106, 109
"Uncle Billy" (*see* Shaw, William)
Union Co., Ohio, 2
United States, 63, 70, 125
United States Army, 26, 125

Vancouver, 65, 84
Victor, Frances Fuller, 133, 134
Virginia, 1, 10

Waiilatpu, 37, 41, 42, 49, 50, 53, 54, 57, 58, 59, 62, 65, 68, 69, 70, 72, 73, 74, 75, 76, 78, 79, 81, 82, 84, 85, 86, 90, 91, 93, 101, 102, 103, 105, 106, 107, 109, 110, 111, 113, 117, 121, 125, 126, 127, 128, 131, 134, 136, 139, 140, 142, 150, 155
Walker, Abigail, 121, 150
Walker, Cyrus, 75, 76, 78, 126

Walker, Elkanah, 41, 42, 53, 55, 57, 72, 73, 75, 79, 121, 150
Walker, Mary, 53, 72, 73, 76, 78, 79, 110, 121, 150
Walla Walla, Wash., 131, 133, 134, 136, 137, 140, 153
Walla Walla Journal, 153
Walla Walla River, 51, 55, 67, 92, 117
Walla Walla Valley, 49, 51, 62, 63, 117, 126, 127
Walla Wallas, 72, 73, 83
Wallula Gap, 65, 121
War Dept., 125
Wascopam, 79, 121
Washington, 131
Westport Landing, 4
Waters, James, 126
Wheeler, N.Y., 43
White Co., Indiana, 2
Whitman, Alice Clarissa, 40, 51, 54, 55, 67, 76
Whitman College, 134, 140, 144, 153, 155
Whitman, Marcus, 7, 25, 36, 37, 39, 40, 41, 42, 43, 44, 45, 46, 48, 49, 50, 51, 54, 55, 57, 58, 59, 60, 61, 62, 63, 65, 68, 69, 70, 71, 72, 73, 74, 75, 76, 78, 79, 80, 81, 82, 83, 84, 85, 86, 87, 88, 89, 90, 91, 92, 93, 95, 99, 105, 106, 107, 110, 111, 116, 125, 128, 133, 134, 136, 148, 153
Whitman, Narcissa, 24, 37, 39, 40, 41, 42, 45, 46, 48, 49, 50, 51, 53, 54, 55, 59, 60, 61, 62, 65, 67, 68, 69, 70, 72, 74, 75, 76, 77, 78, 79, 82, 84, 88, 90, 91, 92, 93, 95, 98, 99, 105, 111, 123, 128, 129, 136, 142, 143, 144, 151
Whitman mission, 27, 31, 32, 35, 36, 59, 126
Whitman, Perrin, 61, 62, 88, 105, 115, 121, 127, 134, 133, 155
Willamette River, 58, 65, 68, 69, 75, 80, 81, 90, 101, 103, 108, 124, 126, 138, 146
Willamette Valley, 4, 30, 36, 37, 40, 41, 45, 53, 69, 70, 81, 115, 116, 121, 146
Willson, William H., 139

Young, Daniel, 107, 110
Young, Elam, 89, 101, 107, 110, 112, 117
Young, James, 101
Young, John, 107